"Bill and Amy have done it again. They have taken the complex and made it fresh and practical—from hard-hitting illustrations to challenging applications. *20/20 Vision* will help every pastor prepare mission messages that will inform and inspire. If you have been looking for a book that shows the sweep of God's purposes for his glory among the nations, *20/20 Vision* is it."

Jim Killgore, President, ACMC (Advancing Churches in Missions Commitment)

"Awesome! Apparently, if you combine a truly professional writing team with personal, intimate (and dramatic) familiarity with exotic places and ministries all over the world, you have a page-turner of both substance and value. Nothing like it!"

**Ralph D. Winter, General Director,
Frontier Mission Fellowship**

"Nobody writes stories about   ancing His kingdom around the world like   s! If you've somehow thought you were   s a Christian, get this book and discove   g in making His name famous among t

Bob Sjogren, President,   RY

"*20/20 Vision* tells story after story of how the Lord used imperfect people in the unfolding of His perfect plan. The book is filled with many useful ideas about how any one of us can have a significant part in the unfolding of the story of His kingdom among the nations. Our risk is to wait rather than run with perseverance the race set before us."

Nelson Malwitz, Director, Finishers Project

Amazing Stories of What God Is Doing Around the World

2o2o VISIOn

Practical Ways Individuals and Churches Can Be Involved

BILL & AMY STEARNS

BETHANYHOUSE
Minneapolis, Minnesota

2020 Vision
Copyright © 2005
Bill and Amy Stearns

Cover design by Jackson Design Company

Published by Bethany House Publishers
11400 Hampshire Avenue South
Bloomington, Minnesota 55438

Bethany House Publishers is a division of
Baker Publishing Group, Grand Rapids, Michigan.

Printed in the United States of America

Library of Congress Cataloging-in-Publication Data

Stearns, Bill.
    2020 vision : amazing stories of what God is doing around the world / by Bill and Amy Stearns.
        p. cm.
    Summary: "True stories of men and women around the world today who are reaching out with the Gospel, plus resources and practical ways individuals and churches can be involved in missions efforts"—Provided by publisher.
ISBN 0-7642-0016-X (pbk.)
    1. Missions. 2. Evangelistic work. 3. Christianity—Forecasting. I. Title: Twenty twenty vision. II. Stearns, Amy. III. Title
    BV2061.3.S74   2005
    266—dc22   2004024642

"Look among the nations! Observe!
Be astonished! Wonder!
Because I am doing something in your days—
You would not believe if you were told."
Habakkuk 1:5

BILL & AMY STEARNS write, teach, and train on challenging the local church to new global vision. The Stearns' experience in mission mobilization, youth work, media, and church-planting has taken them around the world. In addition to several joint projects with Amy, Bill has published twenty-one books. The Stearns invite your feedback—addressed to the publisher or via e-mail to: *Connecting@BillAndAmyStearns.info.*

A *2020 Vision* Group Study Guide is available at no cost at *www.BillAndAmyStearns.info.* This free curriculum is perfect for an elective course in your college-age/adult Sunday school, small-group Bible study, or mission task force. Each session features background commentary, a leader's guide, and participants' worksheets. Designed for the non-mission-minded and mission fanatic alike, the course uses this *2020 Vision* book to explore the biblical basis of God's unchanging purpose.

This project is dedicated to
Zack, Claire, Elijah, and Rowan—
the next generation of world-changers.

ACKNOWLEDGMENTS

Thanks to all the global warriors whose stories are chronicled here—stories all true, even though some are told with altered names or details for security reasons.

Inspiration came from Ralph and the late Roberta Winter and Steve Hawthorne in their *Perspectives on the World Christian Movement* course—from which most of these concepts are taken. (Take the course. Get information at *www.perspectives.org*.)

Thanks to our Father for blessing us with such a moving vision of His heart for the nations.

CONTENTS

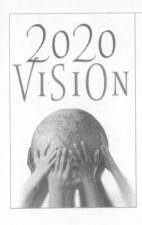

2020 VISION

CHAPTER 1

SOMETHING'S HAPPENING:

What's Not in the Nightly News

To everything there is a season, a time for every purpose under heaven. (Ecclesiastes 3:1 NKJV)

And your time is coming.

Imagine:

Paris. The man in the white fedora and pale linen suit might have just stepped from the set of *Casablanca.* "*Bonsoir.* May I join you?"

You look up, surprised.

It's evening in Paris, cool and drizzly. You're visiting an American couple who are keeping you hilariously entertained with their old save-the-world stories of helping restore the Gospel around the Mediterranean, and you don't know anybody else in this town. That's why it seems safe to be loud. Who cares that you're lowbrow-chic? Like the other tourists, you're all sipping espresso, safely ensconced under blue canvas awnings at the sidewalk tables of the Champs Elysée Häagen-Dazs. Here not even the French waiters will give you the boot for laughing too much.

The fifty-ish North African delicately doffs his hat and smiles through a trimmed gray beard. "So you're the famous Michael and Sharon from America? I think I can tell you the rest of the story."

You look over at Mike and Sharon, whose mouths hang half-open. You sputter, "I'm sorry we were getting loud; especially mentioning the Harratine . . ."

The North African laughs. "No, you are fine. I did overhear, and I think I can tell you what happened to the smuggled plates."

You suddenly realize you're being rude. "Here, please do sit down."

The man settles in, introduces himself, and, in fine Arab-style patience, sits in comfortable silence till a waiter takes his order for a bottle of Badois mineral water. Paris night traffic whizzes by in the light rain. Down near the *Place de la Concorde* a little white police car flips on its klaxon. You're getting impatient to hear what he has to say, but—so very culturally sensitive—you sit and sip your coffee.

Finally he takes up the story. "The last you knew, the offset plates were smuggled off into thin air?"

Mike and Sharon nod at the same time. She says, "I don't know if you'd heard . . . We *were* loud, sorry. We flew in from Venice directly to Zatargat. Fifteen years ago."[1]

The man leans across the little table. "And that is where you worked to restore the abandoned Christian bookstore." He notices Mike and Sharon's guarded look. "Rest assured, I am a believer myself."

Mike still looks concerned. "Frankly, we've been talking too much and too loudly about this. We don't actually know you, sir."

You realize how tricky it is to distinguish a true believer from an undercover religious policeman from a despotic regime; every form of spy from everywhere in the world is in Paris. Wheat or tare?

"I understand," the man says. "So I will tell what I know. The bookstore had been closed because they began printing just a few Bibles and trying to sell them to the Harratine people up in the mountains. The government allowed the bookstore, but not distribution to the Harratine."

He turns to you, since you're the novice in all this. "The Harratine are a minority. One of the Berber peoples, numbering

---

[1]This fictionalized version of a true story alters names, locations, and some details for the sake of security concerns. Throughout *2020 Vision,* some of the true stories are altered in this way, since much of what God is miraculously doing in our world is in restricted countries where proclaiming the Gospel is illegal and/or dangerous.

about one hundred forty thousand Muslims, they are very resistant to the Gospel. Also called *Black Berbers* or *Black Maure.* They've had a New Testament since the thirties, but the church has never taken hold. So unfortunately the bookshop was shut down. Then after several appeals it was allowed to reopen, but no printing Scripture in Harratine. That is when your friends here landed in Zatargat. Fifteen years ago."

Mike apparently decides the man is legit. He says, "That's right. I'm pulling apart broken workbenches in the back of the old bookstore, and lo, and behold, I uncover crates of offset metal plates. We quietly took one to the region's Bible Society rep, and finally figured out they were the printing plates of a newly translated Harratine Bible—the illegal Bible. We freaked! We didn't want to get the reopened bookstore in trouble, yet we wanted the Harratine to have the truth. We've always wondered if we did the right thing in obedience or if somebody lost their life because we tried to save the plates."

The man says, "And so you went clandestine, yes? Contacted some of God's smugglers who then spirited the plates out of the country—a quarter ton of metal! You did well, you two. We talk of you as heroes."

Sharon blinks, recovers, and says, *"Merci, monsieur.* But we've been praying about what God would do with those plates ever since. Fifteen years of prayers."

"You know God's Word never returns void."

"Yes, but what happened next?"

The man's Badois arrives, and he makes a great show of pouring the water over the ice cubes. "They must think I am American," he laughs. "No one uses ice cubes like the Americans." He drinks, then settles back into remembering: "Yes, it is now almost fifteen years since your risky act of obedience in preserving the Word of God. The plates were successfully smuggled to Malaga; no one was harmed or apprehended. Finances were finally raised, and about five years ago the Bibles were printed in Spain on a massive press by the tens of thousands— much more cheaply and in far greater quantities than ever could have been printed in the little shop in Zatargat. It was as if God had planned much greater things for that Bible. A few years ago the Harratine began receiving the Bibles. Since then hundreds and hundreds, and then thousands of them have come to faith in Christ! The little offset press at the bookshop would never have been able to keep up with the demand. Isn't that a wonderful 'rest of the story'?"

"But," you ask, "how did the Bibles get back into the country? You mean someone risked life and limb to smuggle them *back* in to the Harratine?"

The gentleman stands and, like a soldier, puts on his fine white hat. "Well, that," he says, "was *my* job."

You're just an observer in that conversation, but you sense that it could easily have been you helping Mike and Sharon clean up that dusty bookshop fifteen years ago. And then you too would have watched how God expedited your obedience in His plan to print enough Bibles for what He knew was an upcoming spiritual breakthrough among the Harratine.

You. One of God's global heroes—whether the setting is North Africa, Paris, or your hometown.

Today, at our point in history, God is orchestrating across the years and across the globe this kind of gutsy obedience among His followers. His plan for the twenty-first century pulses with true stories like this one as He seems to be initiating what many Christian world-watchers call the greatest revival and harvest the world has ever known.

Something's happening. Something big.

And you have a part in it—even in the near future, between now and 2020.

You in 2020

12:01 A.M. New Year's Day, the year of our Lord 2020. Fireworks. Confetti. Noisemakers. Dick Clark at Times Square?

How old will you be? Where will you be living? What will you be doing?

If you're banking on being raptured by then, sitting with your harp in heaven, think again: Jesus might not have returned by then. The world might still be too much with us.

Imagine yourself in 2020. What life changes have you gone

through? What's going on in your culture? What kind of current events fill the news?

Looking back, you'll see with 20/20 vision what has happened between now and then, what God has done in your life, and what He's done across the world.

But right now, looking ahead to the year 2020 is like squinting through a glass darkly. Futurists with their long-view arts focus on three elements to try to see into the future: current reality, apparent trends, and, of course, the background that led us to this point in history. As believers in Jesus Christ, we can do the same.

In our amateur prognostications, the most solid leads we have about the future lie in our history—in His story. In *2020 Vision* we'll clarify the ancient clues in that story to better understand where we're headed. We'll also consider the trends of what God is doing in His ministry on earth. And we'll see more clearly our current reality—what's actually happening in the world. Plan to be energized by a fresh look at God's Word, His work, and His world—all revealing the big cosmic picture of God's unchangeable purpose for our span of life.

Maybe your heart is restless to be a part of that big picture. Maybe you're restless to catch a new vision of exactly why you're here at this point in history.

Think over the energy you're throwing into life now—trying to be the best you can be, trying to keep your head above water financially, to be a better Christian, a better friend or family member, a better you. Why work so hard? Why ask so often for God's blessing on your life?

If it's to have a nicer, happier life, that's not a bad goal. Especially since that's what heaven will be—an easier, better existence. If that were God's sole purpose for you right now He would simply take you home to heaven, right? But in the here-and-now, biblical discipleship is never described as *nice* or *easy*.

God does want to bless you. But not to make your life easy! He'll bless you because He's got a demanding role for you—a specific task, one that lays down rails to guide your major life decisions, to keep you from spinning your wheels in Christian self-improvement.

Go ahead: Break out of the Christian-culture idea that to

join God's family is to become part of a respectable, privileged group that attends lots of meetings. Being a follower of Jesus is more like being born into a bustling family business—a high-risk business with pressures, challenges, dangerous competition as well as profit-sharing, camaraderie, and job satisfaction. When you're born into this family business everybody takes part in the Father's work.

What, exactly, is the Father doing these days?

Look What God Is Doing

The current reality of our world isn't quite what the prince and power of the airwaves tells us. After all, his job is to deceive the whole world (Revelation 12:9).

As any journalist knows, what makes the news is the exceptional, not the normal. But we hear a news story once, twice, three times—and we tend to think those exceptions illustrate what's ordinary, what's generally happening out there. The nightly news is sometimes a construct that warps the big picture of real life on planet Earth. Most often that warped picture subtly suggests the lie: In the chaos of this world God is losing. If we live and make decisions based on that lie, we'll always be off in terms of understanding exactly where we fit and what the purpose of our time on Earth is.

If we want to be about our Father's business, we won't find out what He's doing from the news. For example, a few items that don't ever seem to be reported in your typical newspaper or media broadcast include:[2]

- Every day another 74,000 people across the globe come to faith in Christ. That's 3,083 new fellow believers every hour of every day. Since you started reading this chapter you have about 100 new brothers and sisters in Christ!
- An average of 3,500 new churches are opening every week worldwide. Thousands of ministries you've probably never heard of are diligently multiplying fellowships of new

---

[2]Rather than clutter *2020 Vision* with hundreds of notes of documentation, the sources for these and all other stories and statistics in the book are listed on the Web at *www.BillandAmyStearns.info*.

believers. For example: In 1991 Gregory and Galina Sukhyna planted the Church of Praise in Krivoy Rog, a colorless Ukrainian city infamous for violent crime and drug addiction. By June 2002 the church had started 33 other churches in the city, a three-year Bible school, a rehabilitation center, and a program to feed the poor. Then in the next two years the movement grew to 400 churches—with another 15 churches planted in Armenia, 45 in Central Asia (nine of them in jails), and others in Moldavia. Galina, a grandmother, has personally started 100 new churches with her team during that two-year period.

● God is using the electronic media: Today there are 1,050 national or international broadcasting agencies producing Christian programming on more than 4000 Christian radio or TV stations. More than three billion people have viewed Christian films such as the *Jesus* film—which has been shown in 228 countries, with 197,298,327 viewers indicating a commitment to Christ!

● More than one-third of the converts to Christianity in Turkey say they came to Christ because He appeared to them in a dream. Professor Dudley Woodbury and a team from Fuller Seminary in California documented 600 cases in which Muslims found new life in Jesus because of dreams or visions. Hindus are dreaming of Jesus too. Manoi, a Hindu sorcerer in Himachal Pradesh, India, served as a priest in the famous Chamunda Temple, which made him rich. But he lost his fortune and so returned to his hometown, where his sister spoke to him about Jesus. Manoi said that if this God existed He should appear to him personally. The following night Jesus did appear to him in a dream, saying, "Today you will become my son." The next day, a pastor "happened" to visit—a pastor who had also had a dream of Jesus. Manoi gave his life to Christ and now plants churches throughout Himachal Pradesh.

● In 1950, when China closed to foreign missionaries, there were one million believers in the country. Today conservative estimates say there are well over 80 million. An average of 28,000 become believers every day in the People's Republic of China!

- Today many believers disillusioned with institutional structures are leaving the church. Yet around the world 112 million born-again Christians "outside" formal church memberships are still very active in outreach and ministry, many times helping to develop new formats of "church" like the "simple church" and "house church" movements.

- During the 1990s the number of born-again believers in the world doubled.

- One denomination striving to keep up with what God is doing reported that a strategy coordinator for a people group in a restricted area in Asia (we have to be vague for the sake of security issues) saw 27 churches multiply to more than 2,000 churches within four years. Another coordinator who trains national church-planters says that together they prayed and set a goal of 200 new churches during his four-year term. When 200 new churches had emerged after only six months, they were forced to change their goal. Now—less than two years later—more than 3,000 churches have been started!

- Every day across the continent of Africa another 20,000 are added to the body of Christ. Africa was 3% Christian in 1900 and is more than 50% Christian today.

- You may feel that few in your fellowship are ardent about prayer, but globally the number of committed believers in full-time prayer ministries has now reached 25 million! Altogether, more than 200 million believers pray daily for world evangelization.

- How are we Bible-believing followers of Christ organized? In:

  - 3,450,000 local churches,
  - representing 33,800 distinct denominations,
  - with 4,000 foreign mission agencies fielding 419,500 foreign missionaries,
  - with 23,000 parachurch organizations,
  - 220,000 Christian primary and secondary schools,
  - 35,500 Christian medical centers and hospitals,

- with 300 church-related research centers—now Internet-linked for instant information-sharing—from which many of these statistics come!

- In 1900 Korea had no Protestant church; the country was deemed "impossible to penetrate." But today Korea is 30% Christian, with 7,000 churches in Seoul alone. Several of these churches have more than one million members each.

- In Indonesia the percentage of Christians is so high the government won't print the statistic—which is probably nearing 25% of the population. The last accurate census of Indonesian Christians, tallied in 1979, revealed that more than two million Muslims had turned to Christ!

- In much of the world, young, faceless leadership is spearheading progress in the body of Christ. In Manchuria, China, one leader of a movement of 19,000 house churches is nineteen years old! On the isolated island of Madagascar, off the southeastern coast of Africa, a young man named Victor led a group of 18 Malagassy teenagers into the interior to an unreached village called *Ambodiudantangena* ("Under the Tree of Judgment"). In the village center stood a pole topped with a cow's skull—the place dedicated for making sacrifices to the ancestral spirits. During two weeks of ministry this young team saw villagers respond to the gospel message as God brought healing and deliverance. Sixty of the 150 villagers found new life in Christ, and they renamed their village *Mahavelona* ("Place of Healing"). And Victor? He'll never make the international news; you'll never read his books or hear him preach at any huge conference. Yet he is one of God's young pillars as He builds His church in this new century.

- The government of Papua New Guinea recently mandated Bible teaching in every school in the country.

- In A.D. 100 there were 360 non-Christians per true believer. Today the ratio is less than seven to every believer as the initiative of the Holy Spirit continues to outstrip our most optimistic plans!

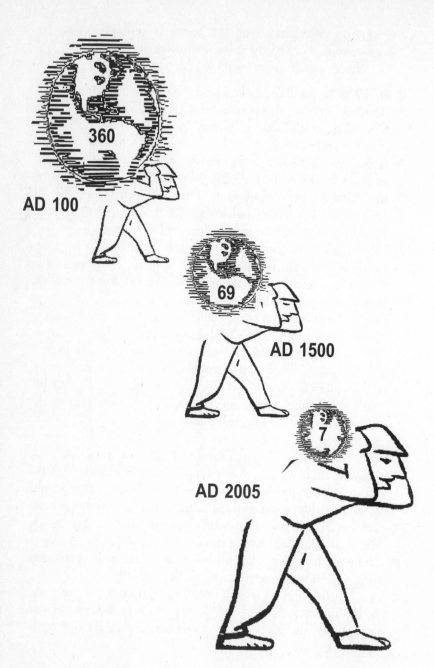

360

AD 100

69

AD 1500

7

AD 2005

Throughout history the growth of the body of Christ has outdistanced the increase of world population.

For every true believer in the early church there were 360 unbelievers. In A.D. 1000 the ratio was 220 unbelievers for every true believer in Christ.

By the year 1900 it was 27 non-Christians per believer. By 1980 the ratio was reduced: 11 non-Christians to one.

In the first years of the twenty-first century the global proportion is seven unbelievers for each true believer in Jesus Christ.

Statistics furnished by the Lausanne Statistical Task Force.

● Where in the world is the fastest percentage of growth of born-again believers in Christ? As of the latest figures available (2000) here are the facts: First is the Northern Mariana Islands (6.64%), then Cameroon (6.07%), next Aruba (5.88%), Guinea (5.02%), and Togo (4.77%). The sixth fastest growing body of believers? French Guiana, at 4.77%. Then Nepal (4.69%), Jordan (4.64%), and Oman (4.43%)! Are you surprised?

● Visited your local Christian bookstore lately? Or browsed through one of the 12,000 major Christian libraries on the planet? You might have noticed that from the world's 2,000 Christian-owned publishing companies, every year we enjoy 26,100 new Christian titles—while a total of three billion Christian books are printed annually!

Where the church has been planted it is growing like wildfire, spreading across geographic and ethnic lines around the globe. God has raised up Surinam missionaries to go to the Muslims of North Africa, Han Chinese believers to settle among unreached Tibetans, and thousands of Indian evangelists to bring the blessing of the Gospel to the 2,000 unreached ethnic groups within India. The Good News is breaking loose worldwide!

And that's only the tip of the iceberg of our heavenly Father's business these days. Just a glimpse of current reality. We'll pepper our *2020 Vision* study with constant reminders of how God is moving today, since an accurate sense of current reality is vital for catching a vision of what's possible in your life leading up to the year 2020.

Get a Grip

Spread out a world map and get a grip on your Bible. We'll sprint through a fresh look at God's Word, His work in His world. And relax: We're not going to scold you into becoming a missionary to Antarctica. Your part in God's historic, global plan will fit who you are. Precisely. Wonderfully.

In all the satanic delusion hurled at us these days, in the chaos of the world, in the roller coaster of everyday decision-making, pleasure, and pressure, the pattern of God's purpose runs from the horizon of the past like a firm, straight road. It continues through your earthly life—under your feet right now as you read this page—and into your future.

You just might sense the shifting of your life's perspective as we consider drawing a line from now right on through the possibilities of the year 2020 and to the culmination, the victory party God will throw for you at the end of your life on earth—which, of course, is the place to start!

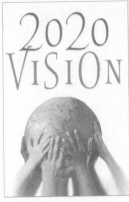

2020 VISION

CHAPTER 2

BEGINNING AT THE END:

A Multicultural Paradise

EUROPE

Turkey

• Bergamum

Bergamum, Turkey. These rocks, slums, and whitewashed blocks of the city used to be called Pergamum—where Jesus sent His message through the apostle John: "I know where you dwell, where Satan's throne is; and you hold fast My name and did not deny My faith" (Revelation 2:13). But over the centuries, the citizens of Pergamum had denied His faith.

And to you it feels as if Satan's throne is just around each corner of the rock-wall warrens you and your team follow out of the city. You feel watched, suspect. Of course, that's part of the feeling of being a foreigner, but. . . . In the glaring spring sunshine and then the sudden squalls every few hours off the Aegean

Sea just fifteen miles west, there's something sinister about the hill you're climbing. It rises one thousand feet from the plain and is home to, in one cleft, the touristed ruins of Trajan's temple and, around another ridge, the city's largest slum. Of course, the hill was also where in John's day the pagans worshiped at a massive elevated altar to Zeus.

As you climb up the hill you could be asking yourself, What am I doing here? But you know it was the SOS e-mail you received from the Russian couple Svetlana and Gorgi. She had written about the business round tables with key leaders in the city and the repair work they're doing to demonstrate God's character in the slums. But it was the following part, written by Svetlana in her less-than-perfect English, that you couldn't ignore:

> Please pray as we go on—we often get very tired. There are so few helpers available that we get very exhausted. Only by God's grace we do what we do now. But we are happy and fulfilled. It is just that we are greedy about the opportunities to touch more people with the Gospel. We are greedy not to lose any of them. Like now during the Passion movie—very popular in Turkey. Gorgi is so grieved that he has so little time and only one body to be at only one cinema two times a day, when he wishes he could be at all cinemas for the whole time. And I cannot do anything to stop my dear husband not to be upset about missing the opportunities.
>
> Bless you guys, let's be greedy for the lost!

And so you came to help.

The project this week is to repair one of the broken-down shacks in the slums, to demonstrate hope in the cynicism of slum life, to work according to the character of Jesus before a whole community. All this while replacing a roof.

All week it's the roof. For the past three days you and a husky crew of other short-termers have carried heavy roofing tiles on your shoulders up a rocky path nearly five-hundred meters to the designated shack. In the heat of the Turkish sun. In the chill of the sporadic spring showers. In the muck and the rocks.

This morning you and the team finally reach the end of the

road up from the city, where it tees in to an even rougher road that runs north and south.

As usual, there are no cars, and Gorgi asks everyone to sit in the center of the wide intersection—a gravel area just below the beginning of the mass of shacks. You gratefully huddle together on the ground under the shade of a scraggly thornbush tree. Up in the ramshackle slum, the children begin shouting and running at your arrival.

"We must pray," he says. "We have no roofing paper. Tar paper. To place under the roof tiles, you see."

You stare out over the whitewashed city: Pergamum, the ancient site of the Temple of the Healing Arts. *So he has us climb all the way up here and doesn't have roofing materials?*

Gorgi is matter-of-fact as only a Russian can be: "We have no money for the roofing paper, so we must pray. Before it rains again."

Feeling about as spiritual as the rocks around you, you silently pray as the team implores God to demonstrate His character to the people of this slum community.

Every day, around the house and along the pathway, dozens of onlookers have sullenly watched each stage of the repair work. Yesterday one of your Turkish co-workers asked among the ragged crowd: "What do you hope for?"

The responses sounded as if Satan were still very much in control of this city. They said, "We don't think about the future, we just live day by day." And, "What can we do with our life? Nothing will ever change." And, "We don't know what the word *dream* means."

This morning perhaps two dozen of the slum-dwellers encircle your prayer session. You look up, and the bony women, grubby children, and old men seem to mock you. Gorgi looks up too as the crowd cackles, and he says in Turkish, "We are praying that God will provide roofing material." He bows again and prays aloud in Russian.

A diesel hum suddenly becomes a roar as a massive Volvo flatbed truck coming up the steep hill downshifts into its lowest gear. In the middle of a Turkish believer's impassioned prayer, you peek to watch the truck bouncing over the ruts. The driver speed-shifts into a higher gear, and the truck is doing about twenty miles an hour as it crests the hill and heads dead-center for your little prayer cluster. The driver blares the horn.

The children scream first, and the slum-dwellers scatter. You're a little slower, and don't know which way to run as the big flatbed swerves back and forth to miss the crowd. It finally veers right and slides across the gravel into a ninety-degree turn, gears grinding as the driver slams on the accelerator to take the road south.

And twenty rolls of roofing tar paper slide off the back of the truck, which is gone in sixty seconds.

The end of a story—especially a true story such as this one—brings clarity. Even avowed atheists, on their deathbeds, can look back on the story of their lives with new understanding, since hindsight is always 20/20 vision.

With God's Word as your guide, imagine yourself at the end of your own life story—at the culmination of the reason you're here on earth. What new insights and deeper understanding from the future might color your day today?

You and Your Life-Span

What if you could be healthy and happy and live to be 100? Maybe with medical advances and a healthy lifestyle, you could live happily and in full health to age 125—along with your friends and your loved ones. Think of the places you could go, the books you could read, the birthday parties!

Now do some mental stretching. Let's say biomedical strides in beating malicious free radicals and telomere loss (Don't ask.) allow you to live with a strong body and mind past the 150-year mark. No worries about choosing between family or career, right? You could raise your two, or twelve, children and then in your second half enjoy a whole new life, studying for degrees in nanotechnology. You. Living to be 150! (What year would that be?)

The first man, Adam, lived 930 years. Adam and Eve's son Seth saw his 912th birthday. And of course the famous Methusela lived to be 969. Think of the stories they told their great-

great-great-grandchildren! Think of what they learned and accomplished.

Some Bible teachers and scientists believe a layer of ice crystals surrounded the earth in ancient days and protected humans from the aging effects of cosmic rays from space. Rain was unknown, but the ground was watered nightly by the dew. Perhaps the world's first rain fell as that ice canopy melted and the resulting downpour was part of what floated Noah's ark in the worldwide Flood. We lost our ice canopy and started to get old too soon, and smart too late. But God originally designed human bodies to live far longer than fourscore years.

Okay. Now work at this: Imagine yourself living those ancients' span of years. You are healthy, learning, connecting, active, happy, digging deep in your relationships with God ("Maybe I'll spend this decade in prayer . . .") and others ("Yes, I've got some time to watch your vacation videos"). You live 300 years, 600, 900 years, and you're still going strong.

Now make the jump: You live happily, in full health, with deep friendships, learning constantly for 1,000 years, 10,000, one million years.

Doesn't work to try to trick our minds into that stretch of imagination, does it? We're so predisposed to snap back to reality. Well, this is reality: One million years from now, as a believer in Jesus Christ, you will be alive and well.

The New You

You will be you. You will be healthy and strong. Fulfilled but yearning to learn more, to experience everything you can. One hundred million years from now you'll be way past your own hang-ups, able to freely and wonderfully connect with others. And finally, fearlessly, able to be infatuated with God.

You'll have a body like the resurrected body Jesus showed us. You will eat as He did, touch and be touched. You'll take up space and time if those things still exist, but you'll not be limited by them: You can appear and disappear into other dimensions. You'll talk and discuss. You'll think and remember. Your appearance will be a little different, but you'll basically look like you—

and you'll be pleased at that! You'll know others, and they'll know you.

You'll finally be able to think! (Right now we're able to use about 3%–10% of our brains. No wonder we're confused!) You'll know so much. But you'll never understand all of God's infinity, so you'll always be learning new, amazing things. In all likelihood some of that new learning will involve God's new, ongoing creations.

As far as we know, God first created the race of angels, spirit-beings who have become involved in and are curious about our human race (1 Peter 1:12). Who knows what the Creator will come up with next and what drama redeemed humans will see in the next era of God's plans? You'll be there to see it and participate in it. You. You as you were created to be, without the myriad effects of sin that now plague your life: diseases, aging body, stunted brainpower, false thinking, and bad advice passed on to you from generations before.

A million years from right now won't you be something?! You will not ooze into the cosmic consciousness as though you were not a created individual. You won't become something you're not—like an angel; you won't sprout wings. You won't blankly sit around on a cloud forever practicing your harp. You'll be your wonderful, glorified self. And you'll be living in a place that Jesus has gone to prepare for you.

Your New World

Yes, we're talking about heaven. The real heaven, where you'll live in a festive garden city—a city that floats in a pristine, new atmosphere over a clean, new earth.

The apostle John saw this place where you'll live—just as Moses in a vision saw the actual heavenly tabernacle he was to replicate on earth (Acts 7:44; Hebrews 8:5). John writes:

> I saw Heaven and earth new-created. Gone the first Heaven, gone the first earth, gone the sea. I saw Holy Jerusalem, new-created, descending resplendent out of Heaven, as ready for God as a bride for her husband. I heard a voice thunder from the Throne: "Look! Look! God has moved into the neighborhood, making his home with men and

women! They're his people, he's their God. He'll wipe every tear from their eyes. Death is gone for good—tears gone, crying gone, pain gone—all the first order of things gone" (Revelation 21:1–4 THE MESSAGE).

The Mediterranean Sea, such a monstrous geological feature to the old apostle John and his contemporaries, will be gone. Perhaps the new earth sports just one huge continent of land and a single ocean—which was possibly the ancient form of our planet before Noah's flood. Some postulate that the separating of the continents occurred after the Flood—during the lifetime of Peleg (whose name means divided), "for in his days the earth was divided" (Genesis 10:25).

In Scripture, the city—the City of Zion, the New Jerusalem, the city whose maker and builder is God—is depicted as coming down out of the heavenly dimension. But there is no description of it coming to rest on the earth. Many Bible scholars believe the New City of Peace (literally, the "Foundation of Peace") will hover like a satellite above the new earth.

It will be a city of peace. There will be no more tears, no more death, no more pain or sorrow, which, of course, suggests that tears, death, pain, and sorrow *will* continue to be part of our lives until heaven. Plan on it.

Your new home will glow like the face of a bride. In the vision John saw of the future the city sparkled in the sun like a huge diamond, like a massive chandelier floating above the new earth.

Looking straight up from the new earth, the underside of the city looks like a square—1,500 miles/2,414 kilometers on each side. But then, backing up to view the city from a distance, you'll see that it's also 1,500 miles/2,414 kilometers high. The New City of Zion is basically in the shape of a cube. About 3.4 billion cubic miles that you'll call home.

Think of the most beautiful place you've ever seen on earth. Remind yourself that that incredible scene is only a corrupted version of God's design (Genesis 3:17; 8:22). Your future home will be His uncorrupted, creative masterpiece; the full beauty of this very real place will leave you speechless.

John does his best to describe Zion in its brilliance, and he does it by using similes and metaphors of gemstones: diamonds (jasper), gates like pearls, streets that look like translucent gold, etc. But later John sees that this sparkling satellite isn't hard, slick stone at all—it's not a sci-fi mass of chrome, glass, and steel. It's a garden.

> Then he showed me the river whose waters give life, sparkling like crystal, flowing out from the throne of God and of the Lamb. Through the middle of the broadway of the city; also, on either side of the river was the tree of life with its twelve varieties of fruit, yielding each month its fresh crop; and the leaves of the tree were for the healing and the restoration of the nations. (Revelation 22:1–2 AMP)

Your ancestors' home on the earth was a Garden with a tree of life. The first humans belonged there, and all of us are always trying to get back to Eden. But God isn't sending you back; He's sending you ahead to the home you long for—a floating garden with trees of life. In the core of the garden city is a throne from which the glorified body of Jesus steps down to talk with you, walk with you as He did with Adam and Eve in the cool of the evening. Now, He doesn't have to remind you that in the Father's household are many homes. You love what He has prepared for you.

From the throne gushes a river of living water. Living water. On each side of the river are forests of the tree of life. The flow of water winds its way through the miles and miles of levels of this garden city—with pathways on either side of the river. Finally, perhaps the river spills out into the crystal sky in a spectacular waterfall to the new earth far below.

Even as glorified humans, you'll have limitations; you'll never be infinite like God. So in this city, as He has done here and there throughout history, our omnipresent God focuses for you the essence of who He is. His presence once focused in the tabernacle, then in the temple. But here in the city He lives with you, and finally you understand it fully: "Behold, the tabernacle of God is among men, and He will dwell among them, and they shall be His people, and God Himself will be among them" (Revelation 21:3).

Does He wander the streets in the form of the resurrected

body of Jesus, with us scrambling like autograph-seekers for a few seconds of His time? Like one of five children whose father can only give you one-fifth of his time, will you feel a bit left out with all these billions of fine neighbors clamoring for God's attention?

No, God is God, and He is infinite. He is omnipresent throughout the city. And because He is infinite in His ability to be totally present with an infinite number of humans, you will walk and talk and be with Him constantly. You'll have 100% of His attention. Just as you do right now—only our current crusty minds obscure that fact. The best part of heaven? Being fully loved by the most spectacular being ever imagined and fully loving in return—one on One.

You've Got Friends

It seems our visions of heaven swing from one extreme to the other. That is, many cults suggest heaven will be just like our lives on earth—only without evil. You get a job, you entertain your in-laws—only you don't fight over dinner. On the other extreme is the idea that heaven is so transcendent, so beyond our comprehension, that it's not "real" in earthly terms—a totally "other" world.

A midpoint sense of life-after-physical-death combines the two. Jesus in His resurrected glorified body gave us a glimpse of how the "incorruptible" is similar to but different from what we're used to. Moses, Ezekiel, John, and apparently Abraham all saw this actual heavenly city. C. S. Lewis pointed out that heaven will be shocking to us mostly because we'll finally realize how solid and real it is compared to our pre-heavenly existence. Yet at the same time the apostle Paul wrote that a vision of heaven revealed some things that are simply indescribable in earthly terms—like not having words to accurately explain a vivid dream to a friend.

But however familiar or magical the environment of heaven will be, one thing is certain: Our heavenly city is filled with people. We'll be among friends.

Who lives with you there? Well, individuals whose names are written in the Lamb's Book of Life:

Nothing dirty or defiled will get into the City, and no one who defiles or deceives. Only those whose names are written in the Lamb's Book of Life will get in. (Revelation 21:27 THE MESSAGE)

Is there anyone you want to be there with you whose name still might not be written in that Book? *Selah.* (An old Hebrew injunction to "pause and meditate.")

God is infinitely concerned with individuals. He's planted in every human His image (Genesis 1:26–27; James 3:9) and crowned each of us "with glory and honor" (Psalm 8:5 NIV). But heaven isn't just about individuals. It's also about groupings of individuals: *nations*—as most English translations render the Greek word *ethne*—ethnic, cultural groups:

The nations will walk in its light, and earth's kings bring in their splendor. They'll bring the glory and honor of the nations into the City. (Revelation 21:24, 26 THE MESSAGE)

Heaven will be a multicultural party. When we sit down with Abraham, Isaac, and Jacob at feasts, there will be people from the North, the South, the East, and the West (Luke 13:29). Bringing what? Borscht. Frijoles. Sushi. Hot dogs. There will be worship in far more than one thousand tongues; perhaps we'll all speak our own God-given languages (Genesis 11:9), and we'll all understand each other. There will be celebrations of what God has placed in every ethnic group that has ever existed on earth.

Every nation, every people group will be represented (even those we're not happy with). For example, imagine how the Jews might have been surprised singing a song about those who would be in heaven, those born again into the City of Zion, including some from their worst enemies:

O City of God, what glorious things are said of you!
I will record Egypt and Babylon among those who know me—
also Philistia and Tyre, and even distant Ethiopia.
They have all become citizens of Jerusalem!
(Psalm 87:3–5 NLT)

A good part of our study about God's solid-rock purpose has

to do with ethnic groups—*nations*—like these. The apostle Paul explained the big picture of God's plan in his message on Mars Hill: "He made from one man every nation of mankind to live on all the face of the earth, having determined their appointed times and the boundaries of their habitation, that they would seek God" (Acts 17:26–27).

Which prods us to wonder: What race were Adam and Eve? What ethnic group? Whatever they were, the hundreds, thousands, and then millions of early humans born would become more and more differentiated into groups. It was God's plan that we all be different.

God allowed the splintering of the human family at the Tower of Babel so that a rebellion against Him would never again infect all of humanity. From the seventy nations listed in Genesis, chapter 10, there have developed though the millennia tens of thousands of nations or ethnic groups. When you study, pray, and agonize over ethnic issues, just remember: God himself is the author of humanity's racial and ethnic groups. He has the solutions to these issues. And when human history is finished, He'll bring us back together—not as one homogenous lump of humanity but as a multi-faceted mixture that more accurately reflects who He is.

No individual or people has its own glory or honor (Romans 3:23). Yet just as God has inserted in each human a facet of His own image, so He has planted within every *ethne* a capacity to reflect His character.

Thailand is a political country that contains various ethnic groups. *Thai* means "free." And when individuals of the majority Thai ethnic group are redeemed, a beautiful spirit of freedom and joy smiles in those believers. They reflect the joyful, lyrical character of our God.

In the political country of Kenya, the huge Maasai people are naturally strong, determined, and disciplined. When Maasai names are written in the Lamb's Book of Life, these believers reflect a different aspect of God's character: His strength, stead-fastness, and reliability.

Redeemed Baluch of Pakistan reflect a different aspect of God's character than do the redeemed Hutsuli *ethne* of the Car-pathian Mountains of Ukraine, who in turn evidence a facet of our Creator that is different from that shown by Kiwi believers in New Zealand, which differs from. . . . You get the idea. God has invested in every ethnic group on earth a capacity to reflect different characteristics of who He is.

If you feel somehow that your own culture, your own race or ethnic group, best reflects God's character, think again! Your crystal garden heavenly hometown needs every people, tribe, tongue, and nation—to more completely show who God is.

Knowing the Invisible God

Why is it so important that God's character be *shown*? Because God is and will always be invisible to humans. And, even glorified, we'll always be human.

God "alone possesses immortality and dwells in unapproachable light, whom no man has seen or can see" (1 Timothy 6:16). Although "no one has seen God at any time" (John 1:18), He does manifest or show himself in visible forms, such as:

- The "angel of the LORD" seen by Hagar (Genesis 16:7)
- The incarnation Moses saw on Mount Sinai (Exodus 33:18–23)
- The cloud, the pillar of fire (Exodus 13:21)
- The Lord seen by Isaiah (Isaiah 6:1)
- The Ancient of Days in Daniel's vision (Daniel 7:9)
- The incarnate, now-glorified body of Jesus—who is the "image of the invisible God" (Colossians 1:15)

God wants us to be able to see Him for who He is; He wants our vision of His every quality to be crystal-clear, 20/20. He wants to be known. God is so "other," so beyond us, such a different being from any of His creatures, that He knows how tough it is for humans to grasp who He is.

If you don't know who someone is, how can you have a relationship with that one?

It's easy for us to mistake who God is not only because He's invisible but because God is not human. He's a non-human life-form; He is spirit. God in His essence doesn't have a body. (He took on a human body in the incarnation, but as God, the God-head, He is not confined to a body.) God isn't in one place or even in one time; but, further, He is not a mere cosmic force floating through the universe. He is a being, a personality with a mind, will, and emotions. In fact, He's not even a *he*—or a *she*. God has no human gender. (Translations of the Word use the pronoun *he* so we don't mistake God for an object; i.e., *it*.) In spite of helpful but always inadequate illustrations, we will probably never understand how one God can be three Persons: God the Father, God the Son, and God the Holy Spirit are our one and only God. God has no age, no face, no weakness. He's not human.

It's hard for us to visualize the non-human, invisible God, so throughout history men and women have often made up who God is. And the mock-up is always wrong, always misrepresents Him.

Have you ever been misrepresented? Accused of something you didn't do? Ever been gossiped about by those who don't like you? Ever had a gesture, action, or word misunderstood and resented by someone? Ever had people reject you before they really knew you? Ever loved someone who didn't trust you? Ever had your heart broken because a person was or is totally indifferent to you?

Then you know how God feels.

The invisible, omnipotent God wants to be known for who He is. This divine drive is so crucial in His relationship with humans that God is infinitely intense—rendered *jealous* in some translations—about protecting and projecting His character, His reputation.

We'll explore later how this fact is central to the framework of your life-purpose.

Nature reflects the character of God and declares His glory (Psalm 19:1). Creation proclaims that He is deity—not human—and He is eternally powerful (Romans 1:20). The instincts He has placed within every human suggest, at some point in every person's life, that He is a righteous Judge who arbitrates what is good and what is evil (Romans 1:18–19). A person may choose to reject that instinctive thought, but God ensures that, at least once, every human considers that there is a righteous God. Two thousand years ago God declared who He is when He took on human form—God in a body: Jesus Christ, "the image of God" (2 Corinthians 4:4). Further, the Word of God—the Bible—reveals who He is (John 5:39).

And there is another way God shows who He is: through humans. He infuses His very nature into redeemed humans (1 Peter 1:3), and we're built to demonstrate His character.

The Registration Book

Now back to the future.

God desires that all facets of His character be reflected in the New Jerusalem, so He wants all the nations represented there. In fact, He's made specific reservations for every *ethne*—in a registration book! There is the Lamb's Book of Life with individual names, and there is also a Register of the Peoples, listing every ethnic group: "The LORD will write in the register of the peoples: 'This one was born in Zion'" (Psalm 87:6 NIV).

Most Western cultures emphasize each person's individuality. But God also deals with individuals in a more "Eastern" way— as members of a group: a family, a generation, a nation. His reservation list of the nations invited to heaven—the Register of the Peoples—includes names you might not yet recognize:

Ahir	Jawa	Lingayat	Mappila	Shaikh
Ansari	Banyumasan	Lodha	Nai	Sonar
Badhai	Kahar	Lohar	Nair	Telaga
Bania	Kayastha	Madiga	Nau Buddh	Teli
Bhoi	Koiri	Madura	Pasi, Hindu	Toroobe
Dhobi	Koli	Mahar	Pendalungan	Tujia
Gadaria	Kumhar	Mahishya	Rajput	Vakkaliga
Hoklo	Kunbi	Mahratta	Sanaani	Vanniyan
Hui	Kurmanji	India	Sayyid	
Igboro	Kurmi	Mahratta		
Fulani		Kunbi		

God has reserved places in the New City of Peace for some from each of these people groups. Around the throne of the Lamb will be some from *every* people (Revelation 5:9). As of today these particular groups for the most part don't even know they've been invited! Yet as you live in your hovering garden city for millions of years, even some from these—perhaps millions from the Jawa Banyumasan people, tens of thousands from the

Vakkaliga—will provide living illustrations of who God is. They—and your own people group—will reflect His character, demonstrating the glory and honor He has invested in them. God's reflected character in us is *actually* His character—not a replica, not smoke and mirrors, but His nature in us (2 Peter 1:3–4). (This in no way suggests, as some cults do, that we will become God or gods. He alone is God; we are not and never will be.) Investing His glory means the spreading out of His character; so an added dimension of God's personal relationship with us will be through each other in our mosaic of ethnic groups. Just as it is right now.

When you look at the nations, the peoples of the earth, what you see in personal encounters, in news reports, in history books, and in the mirror, is every people cloaked in centuries of sin. Disease—an effect of sin—chemicals, and even harmful cosmic rays have mutated our genes. False beliefs have been passed from generation to generation, and we believe our people's lies—from "We are number one" to "Your failure to sacrifice the chicken properly has angered Yama, the god of death." Generations of fear, hate, anger, revenge, foolishness, greed, insecurity, and ungodliness encrust every people group with layers of decay and hide the glory and honor that God has given to every *ethne*.

And yet what God has purposed He will perform.

God will redeem some from every people, tongue, tribe, and nation. And once redeemed, scrubbed blameless by the washing of the water of the Word, like a stunning bride walking up the center aisle, they will enter in through the gates of your eternal hometown. Each entrance will be glorious—flashing facets of God's character. Every *ethne* will finally be clean, pure, and healed: "And the leaves of the tree were for the healing and the restoration of the nations" (Revelation 22:2 AMP).

The nations, and the redeemed individuals like you within each nation, will finally, clearly reflect God's character. That's been on our life-purpose job description all along, but in heaven we'll be really good at it!

The Word is clear about the reality of our brilliant future home, about the diversity of our neighbors. And it's also clear about the reality—no longer seeing through a glass darkly but face-to-face—of fully living out our clean, deep, and personal love relationship with God.

Getting Back Down to Earth

Why have we spent so much time clarifying where you as a believer in Jesus Christ will spend eternity?

Partly because many of us haven't studied much on heaven; it seems so pie-in-the-sky-by-and-by. But mostly because it is "the heavenly vision" (Acts 26:19) that provides the framework for your life. You can draw a line between where you sit right now and that heavenly city, and that's the direction of your life.

With all the talk about life being "a journey" we sometimes think our lonely little road of life is about our individual, personal development.

As if it's all about us.

As if we're just forging on, making our way with God's help till we drop.

As if it only matters that we grow as persons and are sincere about being better Christians.

It's true that God is making us more Christlike as we walk with Him. But He could activate that transformation in the twinkling of an eye if He wanted to. No, our life-direction is not about plodding/racing/skipping through our days just so we learn lessons and get better. Character development is crucial, but—contrary to what some popular cults and some churches teach—your earthly life is not boot camp so you'll be an envied top performer in heaven or get special privileges the rest of us can't enjoy forever.

The Bible suggests that the road of your life is not your own; it's His. He's not making it up as you trundle along; it's already prepared (Ephesians 2:10). And He is with you (Deuteronomy 31:8).

Even in a human sense, you're not alone. Across the globe God instills within His people a pronounced dissatisfaction with current reality. He puts in believers a passionate desire to be "seeking a country of their own . . . a better country, that is, a heavenly one" (Hebrews 11:14, 16). Today hundreds of millions are heading in exactly the same direction as you are, encouraging you with the old Irish blessing: "May the road rise up to meet you." We're in this together.

There's a confidence to our walkabout; we know—anchor-in-the-soul knowing—where the journey is taking us. We're on the road that Abraham—the "Father of Nations"—traveled. "He was looking for the city which has foundations, whose architect and builder is God" (Hebrews 11:10). The Sons of Korah sang about our route: "How blessed is the man whose strength is in You, in whose heart are the highways to Zion!" (Psalm 84:5).

The road to the home you long for passes through wild, unsettling territory. There's very little that's predictable day to day. But we know that it weaves through the homelands of every people group on earth. And we know where it started: in Genesis.

CHAPTER 3

THE KINGDOM STRIKES BACK:

Two Problems, Two Programs

Germany. Fasten your seat belt.

The wheels touch down in Berlin. It takes you an hour to shuffle forward like a zombie through the polished Brandenburg International Airport security and the passport and customs lines to find on one of six unmarked carousels the baggage you over-packed. Then you pay an extortionist's fee for a taxi from the airport to the *Ernst-Reuter Platz.* Then you stagger, jet-lagged, in a pouring summer-morning rain down the *Strasse de 17 Juni* for three hours. That's how long it will take for you and 113,000 others to walk the four miles of this year's demonstration to declare that Jesus is Lord over Germany.

You ask the taxi driver to haul your excess-weight bag to the *Formule Un* hotel—a step above a hostel. It's a French chain; your grandfather never would have believed French lodging would be built on German soil, but now, across the European Union, nationalities and peoples move and travel, study and do business together—which, of course, allows them to more easily encounter Jesus Christ.

You jump out into the summer downpour as the loudspeakers shout, "Jesus ist der Hammer!" Which is slang for *Jesus is pretty cool!*

The music volume makes you cringe; it's the good old '80s classic "Shine, Jesus, Shine," and you belt it out in your own language. Groups of eight or ten hold street-wide banners: *Jesus Tag!* ("Jesus Day!") Early organizers in the '90s decided not to call the demonstration a "March for Jesus," as other believers do in cities such as Sao Paulo, Brazil, where more than two million turned out for a recent March for Jesus. The Germans had told you, "*March* is not a good word in Germany. Had some problems with marches in the past ... So we're calling it 'Jesus Day!'"

More banners proclaim "And You Thought God Was Dead?" Tall gold and blue standards read from top to bottom, *Jesus gibt Leben!* ("Jesus Gives Life!") Your shoes are soaked as you walk slowly in the thick of the mob. It seems almost everyone is twenty-something or a teenager. You attempt your best German with a young man in a hooded blue windbreaker strolling beside you: "I'm not from here, but I wanted to see what God is doing in *Deutschland*!"

He smiles, blinking in the rain, and says, "Happy to have you join us!"

He's speaking perfect English—staccato-like. "*Jah,* I'm Justyn. Isn't this just mad? It's like yesterday. We are giving out the *Jesus* film to thousands of homes and businesses in Berlin this year. Then a bunch of us set up at the mall. Had a sign: *Was bedeutet Jesus für dich?* ('What does Jesus mean to you?') So millions of shoppers are rushing past, and no one stops. We did a cool worship song. Then we did a skit. No one even glances over. I shout out my testimony; I mean, it was ridiculous. Everyone hurries by. So we're all deflated. I go over to pick up the sign, and a woman stops and says, 'So what are you? Hindus? Buddhists? What?' I start to tell her we follow Jesus, and she cuts me off. She says, 'So you believe in Jesus, do you?' And I begin to answer, and she cuts me off again. Then she says, 'Because I would like to ask Jesus in my life. Can you help me with that?' Whoa! Then I think, Oh, she's probably with our church and is just having a little fun with us. But no, she's genuine! So I pray with her, she accepts Christ with tears in her eyes. Then she hurries off, and I haven't seen her since. Isn't it mad?"

His glow is reflected in the faces of the other young believers around you, the 20,000 more ahead of your group, the 80,000 beyond them. Tens of thousands of young German Christians, declaring Jesus as Lord. Thousands of them come from the wild early-'90s movement that came to be called the Jesus Freaks—street kids and blue-haired ex-druggies, finding new life and fellowship in Christ. Recently 10,000 young believers from Germany, Switzerland, and Austria gathered for "The Call Berlin," a simple day of prayer and fasting. Many of the young people had prepared for the Call by fasting for forty days. Some were high-school-age participants in FIRE, the 24/7 prayer movement generated by high-schoolers for high-schoolers in Berlin, Magdeburg, Leipzig, and Dresden.

Verlag ("Down to Earth") is a key new Christian publisher in Berlin. Its imprint, Young Art Edition (Yes, in English), focuses on young Christian artists in print and on the Web, since many new German Christians believe that art is now the primary medium to discuss the deeper meaning of life. British Christian musician Noel Richards counts on the youthful verve of German believers to fire his Olympic Stadium concert in Berlin for the June 2005 "Global Gathering" of 500,000 radical Euro believers!

Yes, this is the city where Adolph Hitler's *Geheime Staatspolizei* (Gestapo) would infiltrate the crowds watching formations of goose-stepping *Sturmabteilung* (Storm Troops) march this same route for the glory of the Third Reich. It's the Berlin of international news, which always highlights the disturbing: Germany will not commit troops; German production is failing; Germany's reformers lock horns with hard-line socialists on retirement benefits; European Union leadership escapes the grasp of Germany.

But this is not your grandfather's Germany. On May 8, 2004, in Stuttgart, 10,000 gathered to commit the new 25-nation Europe to godly values. Romano Prodi, President of the European Commission, addressed the group: "Today, Christians must focus their creativity and energy on ensuring that Europe is not turned into a fortress. Europe is a huge political project, but it can only survive if it has a soul." The legacy of the day itself was significant as evangelical pastor Friedrich Aschoff said, "The eighth of May, 1945, was the day of deliverance from an inhuman, criminal Nazi dictatorship. Fortunately, Christian politicians and statesmen were in the right place at the right time to start the process of reconciliation."

Being in the right place at the right time is now the hope of Target Europe, a strategic prayer network based in Germany and England. This coalition of prayer, worship, training, and evangelism helps unify and channel the commitment of this new generation of believers in Germany and all of Europe. Target Europe's Web site proclaims: "We want to reverse the effects of war and restore Germany, together with the rest of Europe, back to its redemptive purpose for the kingdom of God. We believe that the recent moves of the Spirit exemplify . . . a new window of opportunity for the rising generation to possess their inheritance, to get Europe back."

Even here in Berlin, after decades of division, believers are now working together to take their city for Christ. *Gemeinsam für Berlin e.V* is an initiative of Christian fellowships formed to blitz Berlin with the Gospel—to pray together, demonstrate Christ's presence in Jesus Days like this one, reach out to the country's three million Muslims, and to bless the poor.

If you're not German, it's probable that your mental image of Germany doesn't incorporate much of what God is doing in that culture. Even in this vignette, did you feel your perspective shift just a bit? Hopefully it provides a little different outlook, a little more of God's perspective about 82 million people the rest of us call *Germans*.

Well, just wait till we drop you into a dozen other real-life hot spots around the globe! You'll feel that perspective continuing to shift. You'll find yourself in blood-sweat-and-tears slugfests between good and evil. Incredible miracles. A stirring sweep of spiritual harvest. You'll feel a new sense of the big picture, a fresh vision of God's activity in our world and your part in it.

Quantum Leaps

Being dropped suddenly into a hot spot, frankly, is what your life is about.

Maybe you've studied through Thomas Blackaby's great series called *Experiencing God*. Or Rick Warren's *Purpose-Driven Life*, in which he refers to a key biblical passage: "David . . . served the purpose of God in his own generation" (Acts 13:36). And, like the rest of us bumbling believers, you've gained immeasurable insight on who we are in Jesus Christ and why we're here as unique creations of God.

But since—as we learned after age three—the universe doesn't exactly revolve around us, what's the *context* of our life-purpose? We do know clearly where our journey is to end. But between here and there, what's going on around us?

One of the oldie Hollywood television series rerunning on German television these days is *Quantum Leap*. Remember? The lead character, virtually without warning, is dropped into a hot-spot situation that's a quantum leap from where he has just been. Or he may travel in time and land in another era of history altogether. He has no idea what's happening or why. No clue about his context.

It always takes him some time to figure out who he is in the new situation. In one episode he steps in front of a mirror and sees that he's in the form of a young woman; in another he may be an old fat man or a dirty desperado. It takes some quick thinking to know how to respond to questions, to initiate a next step of action, and to figure out who's a friend and who's a foe.

But there's a theme, a general pattern to these quantum leaps: He is to rescue someone. Sometimes he's confused as to who that is. Usually he doesn't know when something big will happen. And he's always at his wit's end about exactly what to do.

That's you.

You were selected by God to land in this era of history. You had no choice about the timing of your birth, your home culture, or the good, bad, or ugly parenting of your mother or father. No choice about who you are; in fact, it took hours and hours in front of your mirror during your teenage years to try to discern that one, right? There is fun and danger, confusion, humiliation, pleasure, and tumult all around: good guys, bad guys, weird family members. You experience conflict and tension you had nothing to do with and don't really understand. Before you know it, someone's tossing a hefty sack of expectations at you: rules, goals, platitudes, and values that you catch without thinking. You have the strong sense that much is at stake in all this, but you're not quite sure what.

The messy stuff, the swirling *what's happening here?* is what this study is all about. Like most messes, when you back up far enough, you can see some order in the chaos. Like backing away from a huge photograph of dots to finally see a portrait, you can clearly see and understand the big picture of what God is doing in your day.

You have a personal, individual reason for being. It's crucial to explore your individuality, to figure out who it is God has made you to be. Good, so far.

But even if that self-exploration is accurate and fulfilling, the helter-skelter scenarios surrounding your individual life—in which you're a participant whether you like it or not—can still leave you dazed and confused. Or bored.

You have a reason for being part of the big picture for such a time as this. There is danger, evil, love, character-building dilemmas, richness, heartbreak, cool adventure, and the deepest friendships—refreshment that brings rest to your soul—joy, and panic. There's the challenge of a quest that's bigger than you, a clear theme—a framework—for your life that is so solid, so unchangeable, that in the mishmash of your days and years, it becomes an anchor to your soul, sure and steadfast.

You'll serve the purpose of God in your generation.

But it's not about you.

The Bible As a Yearbook

We've all been disappointed: A product doesn't work the way it should. College life is a barrage of stress and loneliness. A dream vacation is soured by problems. A person you thought was extraordinary turns out to be all too ordinary. Disappointment comes when our expectations aren't fulfilled.

Believers in Jesus Christ can be some of the most disappointed people on earth. But we cover it well, don't you think? At least we look good in our meetings.

We can even be disappointed in God—so deeply disappointed that we quit trusting Him. We quit genuinely praying; we believe He'll do things in others' lives, but not in ours. We can also be disappointed in each other. Sometimes the hype from which we built our expectations is so false that we become disappointed with life itself.

In the early '80s the American author Scott Peck rocked many of his "Me Generation" readership with the simple premise of *The Road Not Taken.* Life is not fair. Life is not easy. And it will never be fair or easy. He warned us about our expectation that if I'm a good person and I try hard, life should be good. It's a false expectation, he said, but it's one that we insist on believing.

The Christian false expectations that lead to disappointed lives are labeled by seminar leader Bob Sjogren as "Cat Theology." (See *www.DogAndCatTheology.com.*) Dogs seem to say, "You feed me. You pet me. You shelter me. You love me. You must be God!" Cats seem to say, "You feed me. You pet me. You shelter me. You love me. I must be God!"

A *Far Side* cartoon once depicted a scientist announcing a breakthrough in understanding cat language: "They say only two things. 'Where's my dinner?' and 'Everything here is mine.'"

Even if we're not conceited egomaniacs, we still seem to think the universe was created for us. It's all about me, my relationship with God, my life, my money, my health, my ministry, my family, my happiness, my side of my relationships, and my life-purpose and destiny. As good Christians we study life lessons and identify with the all-time heroes of the Bible: Abraham, Moses, Job, Deborah, David, Elijah, Daniel, Mary, Paul. All good. But why don't we identify with the lesser characters of Scripture: a daughter of Job as she's dying; Rizpah, whose sons were hanged for reparation to the Gibeonites; or the family of Stephen the martyr?

Things may never go well in your life. Ask Jeremiah.

In fact, your life may not be about you. It might be about your son. Or your granddaughter who isn't even born yet. Or about what God is doing in your culture, and you just happen to be in the right or wrong place at the right or wrong time—like a citizen of Jerusalem at the time of Solomon's inauguration or at the time of its destruction in A.D. 70. Or your life may be about some link you develop with the 250,000 believers in Nepal—and just one of them is going to do something spectacular in the next generation—in Germany!

Somewhere in the blush of finding that God is infinitely, personally concerned about me as an individual in His cosmic plan of the universe, I might have become catlike: "Where's my dinner?" I might have forgotten that my role, though significant, is only part of what it's all about.

A cat-perspective is inevitably disappointing because our false expectations will never be fulfilled. (Nobody else in the universe, including God, seems to pay attention to our "everything here is mine" attitude, right?) Cat theology, perhaps, is why the Bible itself is often disappointing. We might treat it like a school yearbook: When we get the new book, we whip it open to see pictures of . . . ourselves! Then of our best friends. It's all about *us*.

But the verses we've underlined in the Book, because they're about us, are only a fraction of what it's all about.

So what *is* it all about?

The Book

Like any good saga, the Book actually consists of a well-plotted introduction, middle story line, and a definitely climactic ending.

The introduction is seen in Genesis 1–11. The middle story line rages with wild conflicts, resolutions, and climaxes that make soap-opera episodes seem tame—which is obvious to anyone plowing through Genesis 12 to the end of the book of Jude. Then, like any good epic, the Bible has a distinct ending—a conclusion—when all the questions and all the conflicts are finally and satisfactorily resolved. The book of Revelation is a pretty unbeatable climax to the story of the Bible.

The outline described above may not be new to everyone, but what may be new is the fact that *the Book is firmly plotted with a single purpose, an unbreakable thread running through the entire saga,* which has the universe as a backdrop and you as one of the principal players. Let's get you prepped on your part in the cosmic unraveling of God's story of humanity and His usurped kingdom as recorded in the Book.

The first lines of the Book are so familiar to most of us that we're apt not to pay much attention to what they are saying. And they're saying plenty. Whole volumes have been written, mostly in conjecture, about the state of the universe as described in Genesis 1:1–2.

Without going into too much detail, as we overview the theme of the Bible, let's look at a sketch of the introduction. Like any good opening, it introduces the lead characters and spells out the conflict:

- *God is an eternal King.* The Psalms sing, "The LORD is King forever (10:16); and His sovereignty rules over all" (103:19). He has always been and always will be in full, complete control. We must acknowledge this fact, or we will never accept our part in His great plan. In His sovereignty He created spirit-beings called angels. He created them in levels of a hierarchy, with specific levels of power and service.

  Philosophers reason that God could not create a being with absolute, inherent perfection or He would be re-creating himself—which is impossible. Regardless of this view, every being God creates must at some time in its existence make a choice to either live according to God's will or outside His will.

- *God's top lieutenant in the angelic hierarchy was an archangel—Lucifer, "star of the morning."* Lucifer ruled God's kingdom in splendor and power (Ezekiel 28:12–17; Jude 9), until his focus shifted to himself. Lucifer decided, as is recorded in Isaiah 14:14, "I will make myself like the Most High." With that infernal vow to live outside God's will, Lucifer became Satan, "The Adversary."

- *The Adversary immediately mustered all the angelic followers he could—one-third of all the spirits in heaven (Revelation 12:4–7).* That only two-thirds of the host of heaven stayed to live in the majesty and bliss of God's presence should tell us something about the incredible allure of this ex-son-of-the-morning! With those that fell with him he began organizing his own kingdom, a rulership to counter and counterfeit God's kingdom. Satan established a kingdom of darkness (Colossians 1:13) with a myriad of loyal, diabolical spirit-beings—who are still organized, powerful, and have nothing to lose.

- *God created another race of beings.* But to these spirit-beings he added physical bodies. Where the spirit and body overlap, we human beings have what is called a soul. God created man. Immediately, of course, Satan jumped in to spin the benefits and features of *his* kingdom. His offerings weren't opposites of God's ideals so much as they were counterfeits. For example: God offered Adam and Eve the fruit of every tree in the Garden but one; Satan offered the one fruit that was forbidden. God walked and talked with the man and woman, sharing with them the knowledge of God; Satan told them the forbidden fruit would give them knowledge. God created man in His own image; Satan promised they could be their own gods.

The Adversary's enticements sounded reasonable and safe; Adam and Eve were not ignorant cave people. Their brains before the Fall were operating at 100% capacity. (Scientists say modern man uses only 3–10% of his brainpower.) The first couple had direct access to the whole counsel of God. They could have chosen to live according to God's will, to eat of the Tree of Life, and live forever in righteousness and holiness (Genesis 3:24; Revelation 22:2). But they opted to follow the god of death. (Just as one-third of the angelic race—basking fully in the reality of His awesome presence—had chosen to rebel against

God and follow Lucifer. This suggests that Satan must be incredibly seductive. *Selah.*)

The devil appealed to man's natural desire to be knowledgeable and independent. He is still an expert at appealing to the desires and appetites of every human body and soul. "Be your own god" hasn't lost its appeal in thousands and thousands of years.

But when humans follow Satan's advice they're following Satan. Although deposed (Colossians 2:15), Satan is still administrating his kingdom as though he were in charge—wherever human beings allow him to be—working with the deception of the "lust of the flesh and the lust of the eyes and the boastful pride of life" (1 John 2:16).

Satan has organized a global "world system," incorporating both his fallen angels and fallen man. This is the system implied in most New Testament passages about "the world." Things are tough in Bangladesh, in Burkina Faso, in Peru, in Azerbaijan, in Wahoo, Nebraska, Dresden, Germany, and in your living room because "the whole world lies in the power of the evil one" (1 John 5:19).

God's Twofold Problem

At this early point in human history, as they say in the old Westerns, "Things were looking bad for the good guys." God's "prime minister" has succeeded in a coup with one-third of the spirit population of heaven, and mankind has fallen into spiritual death and disintegration. This twofold problem presents the basic conflict of the Book.

But God has a twofold program to restore His creation. Part of the program has to do with reclaiming His usurped kingdom, and part has to do with redeeming or "buying back" mankind, who fell under the power of the evil usurper.

This may be a new thought: God's plan is not solely for the salvation of human beings. It also involves restoring His rulership over all His creation—natural and spiritual. Maybe you've wondered: Why did God bother with the risk of creating creatures with the potential for evil, such as Lucifer and Nimrod and Nero and Hitler—and *me*, for that matter? Why hasn't He completely negated Satan's influence in the universe? Why does He allow mankind to suffer in a world decayed by sin? Why doesn't He just solve everything now?

Perhaps part of the answer lies in the entanglements of the twofold problem. That is, the problem of the spirit world being entangled with the natural world of mankind. God's grace in the lives of humans affects the realm of spirit-beings, both God's angels (Hebrews 1:14) and Satan's fallen angels (Ephesians 6:12). Think carefully about Paul's statement in Ephesians:

> I was made a minister . . . so that the manifold wisdom of God might now be made known through the church to the rulers and the authorities in the heavenly places. This was in accordance with the eternal purpose which He carried out in Christ Jesus our Lord. (Ephesians 3:7, 10–11)

"Rulers" and "authorities" throughout the book of Ephesians refer to spiritual beings. Consider the strange intermingling of the angelic and the human world in Paul's admission that he had "become a spectacle to the world, both to angels and to men" (1 Corinthians 4:9). The whole process of proclaiming the news of Christ's salvation involves humans and angelic spirits—"things which now have been announced to you through those who preached the gospel to you by the Holy Spirit sent from heaven—things into which angels long to look" (1 Peter 1:12).

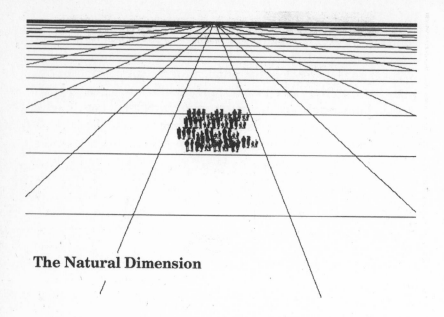

The Natural Dimension

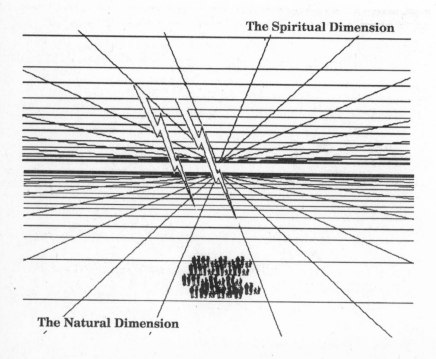

The Spiritual Dimension

The Natural Dimension

Spirit-beings do interact in our world (Daniel 10:10–20; Luke 1:26–33; 1 Timothy 5:21; Hebrews 1:14; Jude 9). And we can interact in theirs (2 Corinthians 10:4–5).

God in His sovereignty is using even the wiles of evil spirit-beings—of the devil himself—to further His overarching purpose for man. And in His foreknowledge He is orchestrating the choices of mankind to further His purposes for the angelic principalities, rulers, and powers. The two worlds are intertwined in their problems and in God's program: It's not just that the devil is trying to get people to fall into sin; he is trying to hold on to his stolen kingship. Sinful man in search of God's salvation is not the only struggle. We are in a constant battle against "the powers, against the world forces of this darkness, against the spiritual forces of wickedness in the heavenly places" (Ephesians 6:12). More is at stake here than man's offensive behavior toward God or our own immediate needs and desires.

It's crucial that we catch the significance of this interworld conflict because it directly affects our part in God's overall purpose.

Until God's kingship is vindicated and until all humankind who will be redeemed are redeemed, God uses angelic rebels and human rebels alike to accomplish His purposes. His sovereignty is so infinite that He makes even the wrath of man praise Him, and His enemies—including Satan and his minions—to serve Him (Psalm 76:10). In a classic cosmic irony, God allows choice; and yet those who choose to be His enemies in both realms end up serving Him in spite of themselves! According to His timing, God is working to right (1) the problem of the usurped kingdom and (2) the problem of fallen man.

God's Twofold Program

As we might expect, God's twofold program to solve the twofold problem is seen in a nutshell in the Book's introduction: "I will put enmity between you and the woman, and between your seed and her seed; He shall bruise you on the head; and you shall bruise him on the heel" (Genesis 3:15). Christ was the seed "born of a woman" (Galatians 4:4) who would be wounded on the heel. And Satan was the "serpent of old" (Revelation

20:2) whose head would be crushed.

Satan temporarily bruised Christ "on the heel" during His death on the cross. But Christ would cast out "the strong man" of this world system (Matthew 12:29). Jesus' death on the cross provided the grounds for Satan's final destruction as well as for man's release from slavery to the kingdom of darkness (Colossians 1:13). He is the Lion of authority to restore the kingdom (Genesis 49:9–10; Revelation 5:5). He is also the Lamb of sacrifice that takes away the sin of the world (Isaiah 53:7; John 1:29). Like Solomon, the most regal of Israel's rulers, and like Isaac, who was offered as a living sacrifice on Mount Moriah, Jesus Christ is Lord and Savior, "the son of David, the son of Abraham" (Matthew 1:1).

Christ's Death and the Twofold Program

In the Spirit World

> Christ's death provided grounds for defeat
> of the satanic counter-kingdom.
> He is the Lion of authority to restore the kingdom.
> He is a regal ruler like Solomon, the "son of David."
> Jesus is Lord.

In the Human World

> Christ's death provided the way for man's release
> from the kingdom of darkness.
> He is the Lamb of sacrifice that takes away the sin of the
> world.
> He is the living sacrifice like Isaac, the "son of Abraham."
> Jesus is Savior.

The two aspects of God's program, as seen in the character of Christ, are depicted in one of John's visions in Revelation. After seeing Jesus as the Lamb and the Lion, John hears an echoing chorus lauding Him as the Savior and Lord of the universe:

> And they sang a new song:
> "You are worthy to take the scroll and to open its seals, because you were slain, and with your blood you purchased men for God from every tribe and language and people and nation. You have made them to be a kingdom and priests to serve our God, and they will reign on the earth."

In a loud voice they sang:

"Worthy is the Lamb, who was slain, to receive power and wealth and wisdom and strength and honor and glory and praise!"

Then I heard every creature in heaven and on earth and under the earth and on the sea, and all that is in them, singing:

"To him who sits on the throne and to the Lamb be praise and honor and glory and power, for ever and ever!" (Revelation 5:9–10, 12–13 NIV)

At the end of time, Christ's twofold purpose will be accomplished as He "hands over the kingdom to the God and Father, when He has abolished all rule and all authority and power" (1 Corinthians 15:24)—referring to the spirit-beings of Satan's counter-kingdom.

We are not involved in this universal scale of myriad events to simply focus on being nice people who do the right thing, serve their community, and go to lots of church meetings—the extent of some folk's Christianity. This is much bigger than that—cosmic entanglements with God's vindicated kingship at stake as well as the salvation of billions of human beings throughout the centuries. God's plan is not a parlor game.

And your part in His historic purpose is significant, critical, hair-raising.

The Tower

The introduction to the story of the Bible closes—as does any good scene—with a climax.

Adam and Eve had been commanded: "Be fruitful and multiply, and fill the earth" (Genesis 1:28). God repeated the mandate twice to Noah and his sons after the Flood (Genesis 9:1, 7): "Be fruitful and multiply, and fill the earth"; "Be fruitful and multiply; populate the earth abundantly and multiply in it." It's pretty obvious: God wanted man to spread out and multiply!

Why command the original couple and the only post-Flood family to multiply and scatter over the face of the globe? Some Bible scholars suggest that if mankind were segmented, it would be far more difficult for a humanity-wide rebellion against

God—as happened before the Flood and after it as well at the Tower of Babel. To keep judgment from falling on all mankind as a whole again, God ordered humans to move out. Over the years, geographical distances would separate them into clusters with different languages and customs. Different ethnicities. In any case, God ordered Noah's sons' families to scatter after the Flood.

In disobedience, Noah's family decided to travel together east from Mount Ararat and settle together in one place—on the Plain of Shinar. Here they built a city on the future site of Babylon (see Daniel 1:2). The story specifies that they used kiln-dried bricks, as opposed to that region's and that era's typical mud/adobe bricks, which can weaken in water. And they used water-resistant mortar. Apparently they didn't believe God's promise that He would not send another flood. And if a massive flood did occur again, they wouldn't have to rely on God's miraculous provision; they could just climb their own tower to save themselves.

Instead of spreading out in the various family groups to obey God's command to "fill the earth," they determined to build a tower to reach up to heaven—to provide their own way of entering into Paradise. "Let us make for ourselves a name, otherwise we will be scattered abroad over the face of the whole earth" (Genesis 11:4) is pretty blatant back talk to the King of the universe, who has just repeated His command to, literally, "[swarm] the earth" (Genesis 9:7).

Will God's plan be thwarted? Hardly. God is the eternal King, the Sovereign of the universe. Thousands of years after this period, Nebuchadnezzar, the ruler of this region, spent seven humiliating years playing the Werewolf of Babylon and concluded:

> [God's] dominion is an eternal dominion;
> his kingdom endures from generation to generation.
> All the peoples of the earth
> are regarded as nothing.
> He does as he pleases
> *with the powers of heaven*
> *and the peoples of the earth.*
> No one can hold back his hand

or say to him: "What have you done?"
(Daniel 4:34–35 NIV, emphasis added).

Notice the added italics; God operates sovereignly in the intertwined spheres of both spirit-beings and human beings.

God's judgment came at the Tower of Babel. He simply pushed mankind into the plan He had had for them all along—to scatter across the face of the earth. God thwarted their misdirected efforts to gain Paradise without Him—the typical goal of world-system religion. Instead, He allowed humanity to diversify.

As listed earlier in chapter 10 of Genesis, about 70 people groups are formed, "according to their families, according to their languages, by their lands, by their nations" (Genesis 10:20). One of these families branched out to settle in Ur, near the northern tip of the Persian Gulf. And in Ur is born one of the most well-known persons in history.

As the Genesis 1–10 "Introduction" of the Bible closes, the first protagonist in the single, core story line of the Bible is Abraham, the "Father of Nations."

For Further Thought

1. Memorize Revelation 5:9. Not only does it combine the Lion/Lamb aspects of the person of Christ, it also focuses on the climax of the story of the Bible!
2. Write a paragraph description of "the world system." Sometime this week explain this concept to a Christian teenager—one of that group who often sees "the big bad *world*" as a joke, as a term describing non-Christian people, or as something "out there" that has little to do with them.

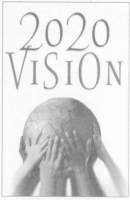

CHAPTER 4

THE ABRAHAM CONNECTION:

Blessed to Be a Blessing

It's cold. You're afraid your toes will never feel warm again. You're bravely trying to drink the hot bowl of *sher chai*—tea with goat's milk, salt, and butter.

And no one has shown up.

Your hosts had set up the evening's meeting in the one guest-house in town, certain that by offering food and bragging about a foreign visitor (you), at least some of the 22,000 hardy Parmiri people would come and listen to stories about *Isa,* the Jesus that even these Ismailis have read about in their Koran.

There's nothing else to do this evening in Khorog, but no one has come.

You're exhausted after a two-day drive from Osh on the head-spinning, hairpin-curved M41 Pamir highway. It got pretty exciting where landslides and avalanches had washed out the potted asphalt, where your Land Cruiser followed mere ruts over frozen mud. But the ultimate breathless segment was over the 15,270-foot (4,655-meter) Ak-Baital Pass—where not being able to breathe was only partly due to altitude.

The Pamir Mountains are known as Ban-I-Dunya—"The Roof of the World"—since this chain of peaks and plateaus spider into the Karakoram and the Himalayas to the south, the Hindu Kush to the west, and the Tan Shan, east into China. During the drive you had focused on the spectacular views, on spotting a snow leopard, or at least an abominable snowman, and on not looking down.

You'd perfected that discipline—not looking down—on your flight from Dushanbe, the capital, to Osh, on Tajik Airlines. You worried about the ancient DC–7, a castoff from the earlier days of the world's most unsafe airline, Russia's Aeroflot. But a hefty Russian steward had assured you the flight that would see you zooming between rock formations and snow-covered peaks was safe. They had only lost one airplane in their entire company history, and that one went down only after being hit by a surface-to-air missile from Afghanistan. "Surely," he had said, "you remember that from your country's fine news reports?"

But none of the Parmiri came to the meeting. Maybe they were suspicious. When the Soviet empire collapsed and Tajikistan became an independent republic, the Parmiri unfortunately had sided with the losers of an early-'90s civil war. So now more than ever they mistrust any outsiders.

They especially distrust the Chinese, their neighbors to the east. And your hosts on this wild trip are Han Chinese. The young couple you'd met in Dushanbe, who had somehow convinced you to come with them to a place no one in his right mind has ever heard of, now simply sit at the cast-iron stove in the guesthouse, praying. Last night, in another lofty guesthouse hut, they had stirred your envy of believers who have a powerful vision. They'd told you how the valiant Chinese church teaches that God has entrusted to them the task of taking the gospel back to Jerusalem. The 80 to 90 million Christians of China are mobilizing 100,000 of their finest, toughest fellow believers to spread the Good News all across Central and South Asia, across the Middle East, and back to the edges of the Mediterranean. One hundred thousand persecution-tested Chinese missionaries. Like this incredible couple.

Suddenly the unpainted wooden door opens in a gush of cold wind. The lady of the guesthouse yanks in an old man bundled in sheepskin and slams the door. A long conversation ensues in a Parmiri dialect of Tajik. The Chinese husband tells you, "Better bundle up. We're going to see a dying horse."

It's now dark outside. Still no snow, but cold. Very cold. You stagger against the wind, following the little trio across frozen ground to a rut of a pathway behind the guesthouse, across a bare field, around several sheds, across another field and a corral of scrawny goats. About this time you can't help but mumble something about "this God-forsaken place."

You finally step into squishy mud inside one of the sheds. The old man swings the door shut behind you, pointing to the horse puffing, eyes glassy, legs out straight, twitching on the ground. Another Parmiri man is huddled at the horse's head; he's holding a huge syringe. The animal snorts ragged breaths.

The Chinese couple pulls you into a circle, and you hold cold hands. "He wants us to pray for the horse. The veterinarian is ready to inject a hormone that will make the horsemeat safe for eating once it dies, and it's dying right now. He knows we are Christians and why we are here, and he says he and his family will follow Christ if Jesus can heal his horse." They bow in prayer.

You're not so fast. You know the value of a horse in this rustic economy: It's the family car, the tractor, and the extra income when it can be loaned out to haul wood. This man is asking whether Jesus will heal the livelihood of his family.

You've also been clued in on the Parmiri's faith: Ismaili, which is a spin-off of Shiite Islam. They have no mosques, no clerics, and no weekly holy day. The spiritual leader of the Ismailis is the Aga Khan, a Swiss-born businessman and horse breeder revered by the Parmiris as a living god.

And now you're going to pray to the true God to heal a horse.

You almost feel like whispering to the couple that you've never quite done this before, but they're already whispering in fervent prayer.

The vet waits with his syringe. The old man looks at you.

You pray, and you immediately sense the huge risk. If you pray and the horse dies, this man and this town that God has *not* forsaken will not follow the Truth. You pray with a vengeance against the powers of darkness, against the diseases that destroy; you ask for the Creator's name to be magnified in this creature.

The horse's breathing steadies.

You peek and see the Chinese couple still frowning in the power of prayer, and you join them.

The vet shouts something, and the horse struggles, flops, then rises to its feet.

We all have heard some version of the laughable "Seven Last Words of the Church": *We've never done it that way before.* And in all likelihood you've never prayed this way before—for the healing of a horse as in this true story (told with altered details for security concerns). But even God's healing of an animal surely is part of the "new thing" He is doing in many parts of the world: "See, I am doing a new thing! Now it springs up; do you not perceive it?" (Isaiah 43:19 NIV).

He's doing lots of new things in Central Asia. When the Soviet Union dissolved in the late '80s-early '90s, many of the new independent countries such as Tajikistan opened up in varying degrees to the gospel message. In Kazakhstan the church is now only about ten to twelve years old. Yet in Kazakhstan's capital, Almaty, Grace Church is running around 3,500 in attendance. A sister church in Karaganda, pastored by Joseph Yu, has more than 2,000 worshipers. As believers shared Christ with their relatives in other areas of Kazakhstan, new churches sprang up throughout the '90s. By 2004 there were 160 Grace Churches in Kazakhstan, with a new one being formed each month.

The second largest church in Almaty is New Life Church. With about 1,500 in attendance, the church hosts CNL, the only 24-hour Christian TV channel in the former Soviet Union. New Life's pastor, Maxim Maximov, has planted 70 other churches in Kazakhstan.

In nearby Uzbekistan there is a church of 5,000. In Kyrgistan, the Church of Jesus Christ has 7,000 members who meet in satellite fellowships three Sundays a month and all together one Sunday a month—a new way of doing "church."

But doing something new, leading us in new ways, is often the way God works—as we see clearly in the life of Abraham, the first hero of the story of the Bible.

The Man

The first eleven chapters of Genesis establish the main characters: God, angelic beings, and man; the setting: earth and "the heavenlies"; and the conflict: Satan's fight for a kingdom and God's redemption of mankind.

God divided mankind into 70 families or nations so the human race could be reached with His blessing of redemption piece by piece; otherwise a unified rebellion against God could again—as in the time of the Flood—necessitate a single, drastic judgment against all mankind.

The call of Abraham, cited in Genesis 12, opens the story line of the Bible. The first three verses of this chapter launch the great plot of Scripture that cohesively incorporates all those familiar, favorite stories as "scenes"—Moses and blood in the Nile, David and Goliath, Daniel and the lions' den, the birth of Jesus, Philip and the Ethiopian eunuch, and on and on.

Out of one of the nations formed at Babel, came the line of Shem, a people who lived in "the hill country of the east" (Genesis 10:21–31) around what we now know as the northern tip of the Persian Gulf. Abraham was probably from the barbarous Chaldeans (not of the later Chaldean empire) or, as some suggest, an Assyrian. Today Abraham would probably have been an Iraqi. Keep this ethnic heritage in mind: Abraham did not begin life as a Hebrew, which simply means "one from across the river"—a term applied to him in Canaan once he arrived as a stranger from across the Jordan River.

In 2000 B.C. God called this son of an idol-worshiper

(Joshua 24:2) to go out from Ur of the Chaldeans, a thriving city of southern Mesopotamia about 220 miles southeast of Baghdad. And Abram ("exalted father")—as he was first named—became the most widely known human being in ancient history, or perhaps in all of history, since Jews, Christians, and Muslims, who comprise a majority of humanity, venerate this man!

Imagine yourself as Abram, hearing the voice of God instructing you to travel west: "Go forth from your country, and from your relatives and from your father's house, to the land which I will show you" (Genesis 12:1). Now, everyone in Ur knows that if you travel west you can go no farther than the land of Canaan—an area central to most of the ancient trade routes formed between Africa, Eurasia, and the East. Besides, your father, with all his herds and servants, and your entire family decides to head out with you "in order to enter the land of Canaan" (Genesis 11:31). At least they'll stick with you as far as Haran, since some of the family had apparently settled there previously ("Haran" was the name of one of Abram's brothers).

But God makes this big step of faith even easier on you: The God of heaven announces, "I will make you a great nation and I will bless you and make your name great" (Genesis 12:2). Translated: You'll be rich and famous—a pretty attractive proposition for anyone!

Is it really that tough to step out and trust this promise?

Abraham (now called "Father of Nations") later grew in faith to trust God when the command was impossible. He and Sarah were far past childbearing-age when God promised them a son. "Without becoming weak in faith he contemplated his own body, now as good as dead since he was about a hundred years old, and the deadness of Sarah's womb; yet, with respect to the promise of God, he did not waver in unbelief, but grew strong in faith" (Romans 4:19–20).

Still later, Abraham acted in trust even in a command that was absurd: "By faith Abraham . . . offered up Isaac, and he who had received the promises was offering up his only begotten son." How could he even think of acting on this command? Abraham had grown in faith: "He considered that God is able to raise people even from the dead" (Hebrews 11:17, 19).

The first call from God, though astounding, seemed reasonable to Abram. He had little to lose, so when God said, "Go," he went.

As the first individual called out from among the 70 peoples or nations of the earth, Abram struck out to start a whole new people group. This would be a people called out from among all the peoples of the world. They would be a people called not after the names of their ancestors—as all of earth's peoples are. They would be a people called by the name of the living God.

Top Line, Bottom Line

The actual promises to Abram pinpoint seven distinct areas of blessing. Think through the passage:

> I will make you a great nation,
> I will bless you,
> and make your name great;
> and so you shall be a blessing;
> and I will bless those who bless you,
> and the one who curses you I will curse.
> And in you all the families of the earth will be blessed.
> (Genesis 12:2–3)

These promises fall into two basic categories. First, God will bless Abraham. Second, through Abraham God will bless others. Who are these others? "All the families of the earth"—the 70 families or language-divided nations formed at the time of the Tower of Babel. These were not politically defined countries; the biblical terms *family/nation/people* refer to a distinct ethnic group separated from other groups by language or culture.

Actually, the second part of this blessing carries the force of a command. "And so you shall be a blessing" could be translated "And so be a blessing." A commentary on this passage by Martin Luther points out that during his lifetime Abraham personally blessed at least seven people groups. Through Abraham's descendant Jesus Christ, God's blessing came to the Gentiles—all people groups (Galatians 3:14)—as He became the payment "for our sins; and not for ours only, but also for those of the whole world" (1 John 2:2). And, as God later announced to Isaac and

Jacob, all of us who are "Abraham's descendants, heirs according to promise" (Galatians 3:29), are to be the "descendants [through whom] all the nations of the earth shall be blessed" (Genesis 26:4; 28:14).

The first category of God's blessing is easily grasped. Sometimes referred to as the "top line" of blessing, it promises that God will bless His people.

Imagine yourself as a wanderer, and for some reason a great king adopts you. He gives you his name so you not only enjoy living in his household but also receive a royal inheritance from him as your father. Then this great, loving father-king asks you to kneel before him, and he rests his great hands on your shoulders. And he blesses you, approves you, vows that all his great power will be available to help you. He leans down and kisses your cheeks and says, "Bless you, my child. I give you my blessing."

That's what Abraham heard. That's what every one of us as believers hears too, since those who by faith "belong to Christ . . . are Abraham's descendants, heirs according to promise" (Galatians 3:29). The Eastern practice of giving a blessing is lost on most Westerners, but we can begin to grasp the idea of the fullness of God's blessing on us from passages such as:

> [God] has blessed us with every spiritual blessing in the heavenly places in Christ. (Ephesians 1:3)

> That you may know . . . what are the riches of the glory of His inheritance in the saints, and what is the surpassing greatness of His power toward us who believe. (Ephesians 1:18–9)

> And to know the love of Christ which surpasses knowledge, that you may be filled up to all the fullness of God. (Ephesians 3:19)

The Book is full of these blessings of God on His people. As more and more individuals in a people group cling to the redemption brought about through Jesus Christ, God promises: "Blessed is the nation whose God is the LORD" (Psalm 33:12). The entire nation or people group enjoys God's blessings!

But the Book is also full of the second phase of God's

blessing, the "bottom-line blessing": *Be* a blessing, and all the families of the earth shall be blessed in you.

Evangelism Versus Social Action?

Some of God's people try to relegate this passing on of God's blessing to the straightforward task of sharing the Gospel. This is the core, the central meaning of God's blessing, of course, since faith in Christ ushers us into God's blessed family: "As many as received Him, [Christ] to them He gave the right to become children of God" (John 1:12). But handing a tract to a starving man is hardly the fulfillment of blessing the nations.

Others swing to the other end of the pendulum of concern for others and spend their time exclusively on feeding the hungry, clothing the naked, visiting the prisoners, caring for the widows and orphans, and championing the cause of the oppressed and the poor. This necessary ministry to the practical needs of people is still only part of the story of God's blessing, however.

How is God's name exalted if a malnourished child receives the Gospel, only to be patted on the head and sent off with a "be warmed and filled"? Similarly, how are we blessing humanity if physical and social needs are met while their spiritual bankruptcy keeps them cut off from the eternal blessing of God's kingdom?

It is clear from Scripture that the church isn't called to choose *either* evangelism *or* social action, as some have polarized these efforts. Others have paralleled the efforts, with the suggestion that both areas of blessing have the same motivation of love, so they can be emphasized as separate but equal ministries.

But we can move beyond both polarization and attempts at paralleling these activities to a prioritization of evangelism *and* social action. Blessing the families of the earth with the gospel of salvation in Christ is received more readily after God's presence has been demonstrated in a people group through social action. Likewise, following a people's reception of the Good News, social action is a natural result to be encouraged.

The "how-to" of passing on the blessing isn't really the problem for most of us, though. Maybe Abraham was like many of us, whose real problem is finding the balance between being blessed and being a blessing!

Balancing the Top and Bottom Lines

When God's people focus too much on the top-line blessing, they eventually become hedonistic. "God bless me to make my life worth living—successful, happy" is a result of a nearsighted focus on the top line of God's blessing.

On the other hand, if they concentrate only on the nobility and sacrifice of the bottom-line responsibility of being a blessing, God's people become martyr-like ascetics. They lose the joy of God's family blessing.

Imbalance of top-line over bottom-line blessings causes us— as it did the people of God through the centuries—to falter in seeing the whole of Scripture. For example, how easily we have clung to "Be still, and know that I am God," but have so often failed to quote the whole verse: "Be still, and know that I am God; I will be exalted among the nations, I will be exalted in the earth" (Psalm 46:10 NIV).

Why do we cut Scripture portions in half to quote the top-line blessings we enjoy as the people of God? We're familiar with "God be gracious to us and bless us, and cause His face to shine upon us." But are we equally familiar with the bottom line of the continuing second verse? "That Your way may be made known on the earth, Your salvation among all nations" (Psalm 67:1–2). Balance is critical.

A top-line focus is almost natural: Humans' old natures are inherently selfish. The "We're Number One" perspective of many in the Northern Hemisphere is obvious in even the world maps used. Most often, Northerners' map projections are based on Mercator's projections, which manage the complexity of placing a round globe on a flat map by distorting the land masses of both the Northern and Southern Hemispheres. For example, the entire continent of Africa seems to be about the size of Canada. North America dwarfs South America:

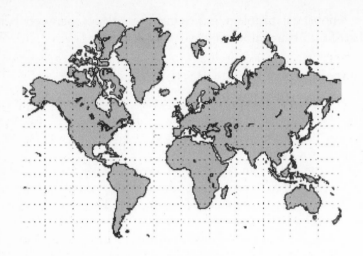

An equal-area perspective of the globe is seen more clearly in, among others, the Trystan Edwards Projection:

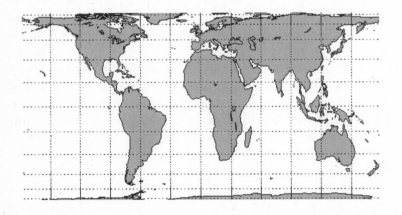

Notice the comparative sizes of North America and South America, the sizes of Europe-Russia and Africa. Even the Mercator-inspired maps in our minds suggest an imbalance in who is more important: those in the Northern Hemisphere or those in the South! (Non-copyrighted maps courtesy of MathWorks, Inc., MathWorks.com.)

The balance is that we are all important in God's eyes. God loves the whole world, not just His own people (John 3:16). We as God's people are significant—just as Abraham was. We are blessed. And we can fully enjoy God's "top-line" blessing. But we're blessed for a purpose: to be a blessing to every people on the face of the earth. And they—even the pre-Christian cultures—are significant as well. The "bottom line" is that we're blessed to be a blessing.

The true balance of this Abrahamic blessing is obviously seen in Christ.

1. Abraham himself was blessed by Christ. Jesus was the Seed of Abraham (Galatians 3:16) in whom Abraham's forward-looking faith found salvation. Christ said, "Your father Abraham rejoiced to see My day, and he saw it and was glad" (John 8:56). The apostle Paul wrote that the Gospel was preached to Abraham (Galatians 3:8)—a Gospel that involved the balance of blessing not only Abraham but also every nation through him.
2. The peoples of the world can be blessed in Christ: "In Christ Jesus the blessing of Abraham might come to the Gentiles [all nations or peoples other than the Jewish people]" (Galatians 3:14).

Abraham's response to the Gospel and the nations' opportunity to respond to God's salvation is seen in the remarkable verse: "The Scripture, foreseeing that God would justify the Gentiles by faith, preached the gospel beforehand to Abraham, saying, 'ALL THE NATIONS SHALL BE BLESSED IN YOU'" (Galatians 3:8).

Go ahead: Count your blessings. Then evaluate each of them as God's gift given to you for a specific purpose. Each is meant to be transformed through your life to become a blessing to every people, tribe, tongue, and nation—including your own, of course.

For example, think about the traveling you're doing from Paris to Khorog: Why has God blessed us with the miracle of modern travel? So we can have better, more exotic vacations? So Grandma can come and visit more often? So you can do business in Sydney and Singapore in the same day? So we can more quickly reach the remaining 6,300 peoples of the earth that have no Gospel witness?

If you answered "all of the above," congratulations! You're on your way to a balanced perspective of the story of the Bible.

For Further Thought

1. Read and think through Genesis 10, tracing Abraham's roots through the genealogies. Remember that Jewish genealogies often skipped whole generations, going from "famous" ancestor to "famous" ancestor.

2. Trace on a Bible map Abraham's route from Ur to Haran to Canaan. What peoples did Abraham have contact with in that migration?

3. Make a list of your "top-line" blessings—the big and small blessings God has brought into your life. Then, next to each top-line blessing, write a corresponding "bottom-line" blessing—a way in which you can pass on some of God's goodness to others.

   For example, if God has gifted you with skills in computer programming, how is that not only a blessing for you but also a potential blessing for others? Perhaps because of a difficulty in your life God has blessed you with extra free time. What's the bottom-line potential of that blessing?

   Blessing others in your own people group is necessary and fulfilling. But a tougher challenge is to go over your top-line blessings list and determine how to pass on some of that blessing to *another people group*!

4. Share the top-line/bottom-line concept with a friend. Don't push the bottom-line responsibility to bless every people as your chance to dump guilt on your friend, but challenge him or her to help you in realizing your own top-line/bottom-line blessings as suggested above.

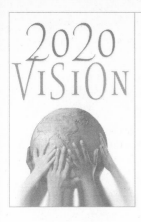

CHAPTER 5

THE MASTER STRATEGY:

God's Unchangeable Purpose

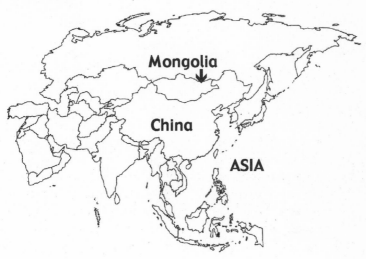

Must be jet lag; you've never fallen asleep getting a haircut before. But in the bright sunshine, you're awake now. The young Mongolian woman cutting your hair is talking as if you've been listening all along.

"Yes, the church in Erdenet started with fourteen of us teenage girls in '93. Then, with all the training, we sent out two church-planting teams seven years later, and I came with this team to the Darhad people. When we arrived in the wintertime in February, everyone told us to go home, that they were shamanistic and did not want foreign gods. They had run off the local Buddhist priest, and their officials tried to discourage us. So we prayed for a strategy."

"Cutting hair?" you ask. You're looking out over what seems like miles of wild flowers, with mountains to the north and stands of pine finally merging into a mass of forest up the slopes of the foothills. Rinchinlkhumbe *soum* (county) is famous for its beauty. The sky is cobalt-blue, and the sun—the sun that shines about three hundred days of the year—is blinding on the white sheet around your shoulders. Yes, your haircut is taking place outside on the back porch of what you'd call a log cabin. And you have an audience of bright, grinning Mongol children.

"No, we sensed God telling us to go first to the poorhouse. It's an actual house, a big Soviet-style building, for the homeless. Someone told us the poor there had not cleaned the building or the compound around it for at least twelve years! No matter how the government threatened, they wouldn't lift a finger to clean up the mess. But these destitute people became very excited about Jesus Christ, and several came to the Lord. And the atmosphere of the place changed. An entire family was saved that May. And soon enough one of the new believers began saying, 'We are new creations! Children of the only true God! We cannot live like this!' And they and we worked and worked to clean the place—even digging up old pits of waste around the compound. The community was amazed: 'This must be a powerful God. He did what no one, not even the government or the law could do!' Would you like more off the back?"

You'd almost forgotten you were getting a haircut as you imagine the poorhouse scene. "Yes."

"The governor of Khuvsgul Province heard of the transformation and visited us. He listened to our message of Christ. Then he said, 'This is very good. I will summon the whole population and command them to join you in your religion!'" Your hairdresser stops to laugh—the pure, bright happiness of redeemed Mongolian laughter. These young Christians simply glow. "But we told him it might be best if the people decided on their own, and yet we would appreciate the freedom to work and preach here. That's where the haircutting came in; this is how I earn my living, and it's a perfect time to talk about Jesus! Our other business is a new public shower house, since no one in the town has showers in their homes, and the old shower house was condemned long ago by the health department. So we've been cutting hair and cleaning shower stalls and building the kingdom!"

You learn more of the story: When there were just 20 people in this fledgling church, these new believers began—in their poverty—practicing stewardship and giving. They were soon able to send an entire family to Khatgal on the shores of Lake Khuvsgul. Just three years after the Mongolians from Erdenet brought the Gospel to the Darhads in Rinchinlhube, this family established a church with 20 believers in Khatgal. A second church-plant was also launched from the Darhad church—with the leader from the Erdenet team leading a new team in planting a third congregation in Moron, in the center of the province. All this within three years!

This simple progression of the kingdom represents what God is doing in this far-flung corner of this remote country. What's happened in the central cities—Ulaan Bataar, the capital, or Erdenet—is even more stunning. From possibly one believer in 1990, the church mushroomed to about 30,000 Christians by 2004.

The beginning of the Mongolian church occurred, of course, in Tanzania, Africa. Or perhaps on a bear hunt. Then again, maybe it was during a rodeo of Native Americans. Only God could launch the gospel in Mongolia in such a strange, miraculous way—which is typical for Him:

In the 1870s Swedish missionaries arrived in Mongolia— what was called "Outer Mongolia." After four decades of several teams' blood, sweat, and tears, not a single indigenous church had been established. Then in 1921 Mongolia earned the dubious distinction of being the only country in the world to voluntarily invite the Soviets to bring communism to their country. In the ensuing purge, every vestige of Christianity, as well as any other religion, was erased; more than one million Lamaistic Buddhist priests were slaughtered. Religion was dead in Mongolia.

In 1980 a young Mongolian whom we'll call Yi (Mongolians traditionally have only one name) went to study at a university in Moscow. Yi received an English-language Bible from a fellow student from Tanzania. "You can study English with it," the

Tanzanian student had explained. Yi then studied the Word for seven years, returning to Mongolia and rising to a top English interpreter position with the government. In 1987 Yi was assigned to an American big-game tourist group, which had come to Mongolia to hunt bear. Doug Coe, a Christian, was one of the tourists.

During the hunting trip Yi found the opportunity to secretly ask Doug, "Do you know God?" Doug nodded.

Three hours later, Yi was able to whisper, "What is His name?"

"Jesus Christ."

In bits and pieces of stolen conversations throughout the rest of the big-game hunt, Doug was able to introduce Yi to Jesus. "Don't worry," he told Yi. "I know it's illegal to be a Christian, and it will be hard for you. But friends will come." Then the foreign hunters left Mongolia.

Three years later Yi was assigned to another foreign tour group—a cowboy team of Navajo, Winnebago, Cocapaw, and other Native Americans who came to Mongolia to perform in the national *nadim,* a competition in horsemanship. Of course, the group was a *Christian* Native American cowboy team. So Yi translated their testimonies on national TV and interpreted their explanation of the Gospel to press groups and officials. Several Mongolians responded to the team's challenge to receive Christ, and Yi spent hours and hours drinking in everything the team knew about the Word. Then they too had to leave Mongolia.

Yi began discipling those who'd come to Christ through the cowboys' ministry.

Then another tour group came, a few members of which happened to be pastors. The ministers, after days of intense discipling, realized the depth of Yi's Bible knowledge and the unusual bursts of his spiritual insights. So they all gathered in a hotel room in Ulaan Bataar one very cold day in November 1990 and ordained Yi as an elder of the first Mongolian church in the history of the world!

But Mongolia isn't the only Far Eastern area where God is lavishly pouring out His blessing.

Another obvious hot spot of God's activity is China—the

economic and political powerhouse that has led some to predict that this will be "The Chinese Century." The shift from a hardline Communist economic structure to a reformed acceptance of limited capitalism portends increasing freedoms in China. Very possibly, one day soon, the leadership of the People's Republic will realize that their 50-year-old war on Christianity is costing more than it is profiting, that they are losing that war. For example, in the 1960s Wenzhou City, in Zhejiang Province, was selected as a model for the campaign for renouncing religion. Today it is the most Christian city in China, with Christians officially numbering 300,000, according to *Operation World*. (See Resources at the back of this book.) In the international glare of its new membership in the World Trade Organization and its hosting of the 2008 Olympics, the leadership of China might realize that the Church of Jesus Christ is not an enemy to be destroyed.

Broader freedom of religion for the Chinese will mean that tens of millions of wise veterans of suffering can unleash their ministries openly. *Newsweek* magazine in its May 10, 2004, issue concluded an article on the house church movement:

> A flourishing church could solve a lot of problems for China's leaders. In some places officials look the other way as churches open orphanages, elder-care homes, and other badly needed services. But even if Beijing doesn't allow real religious freedom, Chinese Christians will continue to spread the Word at home and abroad.

And *abroad* fits precisely the visionary legend of the Chinese body of Christ.

In A.D. 33 the focus of God's outpouring of His blessing to bless every people centered in Jerusalem. The power of the Gospel spread out from Jerusalem along the trade routes. Some Christians voluntarily moved out to bless other nations. Others went involuntarily when persecution struck Jerusalem (Acts 8:1). Then hundreds of years later the focus shifted to Rome. More blessing seemed to accompany God's people, and even bolder outreach took the Gospel as far as Mongolia. Then Western Europe was blessed as a key focus of God's outpouring, and the race to bless all nations intensified. Hundreds of years later

North America seemed to be especially blessed by God, and the Good News radiated out in unprecedented power. None of these locations reduced what God was doing in other parts of the world, of course; there just seemed to be a special expansion of God's global plan bursting forth from these regions. Many Christian world-watchers now feel that the focus of God's out-pouring is shifting again—toward China and the Far East. For decades the persecuted yet blossoming Chinese church has taught that its mandate is to carry the Gospel back to Jerusalem. Chinese believers are praying that millions of men and women across Central Asia, Afghanistan, the Sub-Continent, and the Middle East will come to faith in Christ as the Chinese church gears up in its "Back to Jerusalem" movement.

Chinese house church leaders put it this way on the Web site *(www.BacktoJerusalem.com):*

> The Back to Jerusalem vision is something that thousands of Chinese Christians are willing to die for. The vision is a passion for the house churches of China. We pray about it daily, dream about it, and talk about it over break-fast, lunch and dinner. The Back to Jerusalem vision is not some small trivial matter for us, but the driving force of our lives and ministries. Many feel it is God's ultimate call and destiny for the Chinese Church, the very reason they exist! BTJ refers to a call from God for the Chinese Church to preach the Gospel and establish fellowships of believers in all the countries, cities, towns, and ethnic groups between China and Jerusalem. This vision is no small task, for within those nations lay the three largest spiritual strong-holds in the world today that have yet to be conquered by the Gospel: the giants of Islam, Buddhism, and Hinduism.
>
> We hope you will be encouraged and challenged by the Back to Jerusalem vision, and moved to prayer and involve-ment in the fulfillment of the Great Commission in these last days, until "the kingdom of the world has become the kingdom of our Lord and of his Christ, and He will reign forever and ever" (Revelation 11:15).

God knew that in the suffering and persecution of His fol-lowers in China, and in the helter-skelter of our lives, we all desperately need something stable and predictable to hold on to;

to hope toward; to be confident about, like an anchor in our souls. So He repeated himself.

Repeated Repetitions

The story is told of Carl Sandburg, the great American poet, who as a college student took his roommate home to visit for the holidays. As Carl introduced his roommate to his hard-of-hearing aunt, he announced, "Auntie, I want you to meet my roommate, Al Specknoodle!" The aunt cupped her ear and shook her head. Carl tried again: "I want you to meet my roommate, Al Specknoodle!" The aunt frowned and shook her head again. Carl sputtered and shouted, "Al Specknoodle! My roommate!" Finally the aunt burst into tears; "It's no use, Carl," she said. "No matter how many times you say it, it still sounds like Al Specknoodle!"

No matter how many times or how obviously God has announced His clear purpose on earth to bless every people, it seems His people never quite get the message. We keep thinking that the "bottom-line" part of the promise isn't as important as the "top line," which has to do with blessing us, His people. Because we are, of course, more important than they are, right?

God knows our dullness of hearing. So He very meticulously repeats His twofold promise a full five times in the book of Genesis.

As God was about to destroy Sodom and Gomorrah, He said, "Abraham will surely become a great and mighty nation, and in him all the nations of the earth will be blessed" (Genesis 18:18).

Then God again repeated the promise after Abraham's offering of his son, Isaac—who was the initial fulfillment of the promise: "'By Myself I have sworn, declares the LORD, because you have done this thing . . . indeed I will greatly bless you, and . . . in your seed all the nations of the earth shall be blessed'" (Genesis 22:16–18).

So far God has added the adverbs *surely* and *indeed*. It sounds like He means business. Later God repeats the promise to Isaac: "I will multiply your descendants . . . and by your descendants all the nations of the earth shall be blessed" (Genesis

26:4). Not only would the Seed of Abraham, Jesus Christ himself (see Galatians 3:14, 16), shed His blood to offer blessing to the peoples of the earth; also all the descendants of Abraham and Isaac would bless the nations. Who are these descendants? The New Testament is clear:

> The children of the promise are regarded as descendants. (Romans 9:8)
> You, brethren [Galatian believers from non-Jewish peoples], like Isaac, are children of promise. (Galatians 4:28)
> If you belong to Christ, then you are Abraham's offspring, heirs according to promise. (Galatians 3:29)

Jot it down somewhere obvious, where it can be seen repeatedly throughout the day: We who belong to Christ fit precisely into God's repeated promise that by us—Abraham's and Isaac's descendants by faith—all the nations of the earth shall be blessed!

Then God again repeated His promise to Jacob in his dream while he slept on a rock pillow at Bethel: "Your descendants shall also be like the dust of the earth . . . and in you and in your descendants shall all the families of the earth be blessed. Behold, I am with you" (Genesis 28:14–15). (The initial clause in verse 15 in the Septuagint—the ancient Greek translation of the Old Testament from which Jesus often quoted—is "Lo, I am with you always." We'll come back to this point later in our sprint through the New Testament.)

Have you ever wondered why the Bible so often identifies the Lord as the God of "Abraham, Isaac, and Jacob"? If you search the biographies of these men's lives you will see that the reason cannot be based on their sterling righteousness or faultless behavior. Wouldn't it make more sense for God to identify himself as the God of more spectacular figures, such as Enoch, Elijah, or John the Baptist?—the God of Moses, David, and Jeremiah?

But God is the God of Abraham, Isaac, and Jacob because it was to these three that the twofold promise was given. That's how important the "blessed to be a blessing" principle is: God wanted His name identified with it.

Eventually Abraham, Isaac, and Jacob will actually see both

levels of God's promise fulfilled. They will sit down at a great banquet and "many will come from east and west, and recline at the table with Abraham, Isaac and Jacob" (Matthew 8:11). Luke adds that these will come not only from the east and west but from the north and south as well (Luke 13:29)—from all over the globe! Our God is the God of Abraham, Isaac, and Jacob because it was to these men He gave His promise to redeem some from every people, tribe, tongue, and nation.

But we skipped over something a little astounding: God swore.

We may think it would only be from the mouth of a carnal Christian that we would ever hear a determined "By God, I'm going to . . ." When a person means business, it almost seems natural, in any language, to swear "by the gods."

When God means business, He of course can swear by no name greater than His own. So to shockingly underscore His determination, God himself swears to Abraham, "By Myself I have sworn, declares the LORD . . . indeed I will greatly bless you, and . . . in your seed all the nations of the earth shall be blessed, because you have obeyed My voice" (Genesis 22:16–18).

The writer of Hebrews picks up on this amazing incident and tells us it can be the most encouraging thing that we can hold on to in our helter-skelter lives on earth. God's sworn promise to Abraham can help us to "show the same diligence so as to realize the full assurance of hope until the end" (Hebrews 6:11).

To most of us believers the topic of assurance usually prompts us to reaffirm our personal commitment to Christ for salvation. If you sense a lack of assurance, you probably aren't certain you're headed for heaven. So the counsel given is almost always to make sure you've made that specific commitment to Jesus Christ as your personal Lord and Savior; that process does bring a sense of assurance.

But the writer of Hebrews is talking about an even more effective assurance—[so that] "we who have taken refuge would have strong encouragement to take hold of the hope set before us. This hope we have as an anchor of the soul, a hope both sure and steadfast" (Hebrews 6:18–19).

What brings that "anchor-of-the-soul" kind of assurance in

our lives? How do we sense that stability? Think through the verses between the verse on "full assurance" (6:11) and the one about "hope both sure and steadfast" (6:19).

"When God made the promise to Abraham, since He could swear by no one greater, He swore by Himself saying, 'I WILL SURELY BLESS YOU AND I WILL SURELY MULTIPLY YOU' " (Hebrews 6:13–14). God promised that *by Himself* He would bless Abraham with an heir. And did He come through with His promise?

"And so, having patiently waited, he obtained the promise" (Hebrews 6:15). It's a pretty simple formula: God swears to do something, Abraham believes Him, and the promise is fulfilled. Looking back on that pattern later must have brought Abraham great assurance that God was indeed—even when things were biologically impossible—going to come through for him. He could count on God. And so Abraham lived another full seventy-five years in solid hope, "breathed his last and died in a ripe old age, an old man and satisfied with life" (Genesis 25:8).

Why do we often worry about whether God will come through for us? Why can't we spend the "last" seventy-five years of our lives in solid confidence of His working in our lives and feel deeply satisfied with life? Perhaps because somehow we've gotten the idea that God is supposed to respond to our pleas, to what we feel are our needs. And often He doesn't. We become disappointed with Him and—perhaps without ever hinting at such blasphemy—feel that He's unreliable. The prophet Jeremiah felt exactly that way in his life of troubles; he complained to God, "Will You indeed be to me like a deceptive stream with water that is unreliable?" (Jeremiah 15:18). The King James Version of that passage puts it about as forcefully as a translator would dare when speaking to God: "Wilt thou be altogether unto me as a liar, and as waters that fail?"

Many people who reject God, even when raised in a Christian environment, can point back to a specific event that convinced them that God—if God exists at all—is unreliable. They've prayed that God would save the life of a loved one, and the person dies. They experience a horrible personal trauma and God doesn't rescue them; therefore they feel that God doesn't care. Even some Christians live the life of a practical atheist.

They know He exists and has saved them, but they frankly don't trust Him because He has "let them down."

But maybe it's time for us to get scriptural in our expectations of God's reliability. He won't always do what we think He should do. But He will always do exactly what He says He will do. And on this we can base a whole new life of confident assurance, of encouraging hope. God will do what He set out to do, and as we align with that, we have steadfastness and sureness like an anchor of the soul—even through tough times of doubt and tragedy.

So what has God said He would do?

He said He would give Abraham an heir; and He did.

Now look carefully at the second solid, unchangeable thing God swore He would do:

> In the same way God, desiring even more to show to the heirs of the promise the unchangeableness of His purpose, interposed with an oath, so that by two unchangeable things in which it is impossible for God to lie, we who have taken refuge would have strong encouragement. (Hebrews 6:17–18)

The first unchangeable thing God swore about was that He would bless Abraham with a son. That was the basis of Abraham's patient, confident hope. The second unchangeable thing God swore about was that He would through Abraham's heirs bless every people group on the face of the earth. It's as if four thousand years ago God swore, "By God, I will bring My salvation to the Darhad people of northern Mongolia." His offer of blessing to the Darhad was not a matter of "if" but "when, how, and through whom."

God's promise was twofold, and He swore that He would accomplish both parts of His covenant. He wanted to convince Abraham of His blessing, and yet He desires even more to show to us believers—the heirs of the promise (Galatians 3:29)—that He will, through us, bless all the nations.

His twofold program is unchangeable. He wants us to be assured of "the unchangeableness of His purpose." That we are blessed to be a blessing to every people group comprises "two unchangeable things." And as we align our worldview and our lives with that solid-as-a-rock purpose we will have an uncanny confidence in Him, a goal to look forward to with hope that is "steadfast and sure."

Imagine that you step on a train bound for Bucksnort, Tennessee, in the United States. The tracks under your coach run nowhere but straight into Bucksnort. (Yes, it's an actual town in Tennessee!) The train will stop in Bucksnort at the end of its run. You overheard the engineer swear to the railroad owner himself: "By God, we're going to Bucksnort!" Even if you don't know the territory, even if you're not quite sure of the way to Bucksnort yourself, even if there seem to be a lot of stops and starts and clanging and black nights along the way, couldn't you relax a bit with a sense of assurance that you would eventually arrive in Bucksnort?

Relax. Slip into your own niche in God's big-picture plan of blessing every nation with the news of redemption in Christ. The way might involve periods of darkness, discomfort, irritation, and impatience. But as you align your life with God's unchangeable purpose to be blessed and in turn to bless the nations, you know where you're going. You know what He's doing. You can go confidently about your Father's business.

Go ahead. Realize the full assurance of hope. Have a good dose of strong encouragement. Lay hold of the hope that is set before you. Sense that anchor in your soul and enjoy a hope sure and steadfast. Maybe you and your fellowship can grow to the vibrancy and power of the church in Mongolia, or the church in China!

For Further Thought

1. Meditate on Hebrews 6:11–18. Dwell on the implications of God declaring His unchangeable purpose—His twofold promise to (a.) bless Abraham and his descendants, and (b.) through them bless every people group. How can these "two unchangeable things" on which God staked His own name become your own sure and steadfast "anchor of the soul"? If this were the focus of your life, your church, or your fellow-

ship, what changes might you see? Make a list.
2. Share the encouragement of having hope even beyond the step of personal salvation with a friend who is struggling with purpose in life.

2020
VISION

CHAPTER 6

SO YOU'RE ENTERING THE PRIESTHOOD:

Obligation and Opportunity

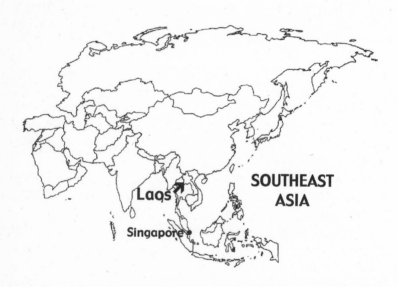

Laos

Singapore

SOUTHEAST ASIA

Singapore. You awake, ears still buzzing from your quantum leap from the peasant huts of China to clean, ultramodern Singapore. Swinging back the white curtains of your thirty-seventh-floor hotel room, you survey the bright, bustling city-state where an official 15% are Christians—though among the educated and professionals, the percentage is higher. More than 41% of university students and 73% of medical students are Christians.

At breakfast on a patio near the hotel pool, you begin chatting with an older American couple. She introduces herself as

Mertie; she's everyone's grandmother—hair in a gray bun, sweet smile, and all. He's Ernie, distinguished with an impeccable white mustache. You find they're experts on Southeast Asia, a result of decades of work as missionaries to the Meo people in Laos—called the Hmong in Vietnam, Thailand, and China.

Under the brilliant patio sunshine, over your eggs Benedict, you're briefed on how God determined it was time to bless the Meo.

It was May 1950. Disappointed with lack of results, a missionary family trying to reach the Meo left their village for a mission conference in Vietnam. They asked Kheng, a young Khmu tribesman from the province of Luang Prabang, to oversee their house while they were away. Kheng, a believer "foreign" to the Meo, was a zealous Christian and immediately went about the village telling people about Christ.

On several occasions Kheng noticed a weather-worn old man, dressed in the traditional garb of a Meo shaman, listening intently to his stories of Jesus and the God who sent Him. One afternoon Bo-Si, the shaman, motioned for Kheng. Years before, he told Kheng, a woman shaman in another Meo village had prophesied that in three years a man would come to tell their people about the True God.

"I am convinced," said Bo-Si, "that you, Kheng, are the one prophesied about. And this *Yesu* of whom you speak is Fua-Tai, the Lord. He is the One sent by the One True God!"

Kheng was taken by Bo-Si to his village, where the chief led the entire group to express faith in *Fua-Tai Yesu* (the Lord Jesus, in the Meo language). Kheng was then taken to the village of the woman shaman who had three years earlier made the prediction of his coming. After listening to Kheng's story, she declared emphatically that this was indeed the One True God and led her entire village in professing Jesus.

Soon other villages in the area, who also knew of the prophecy, sent for Kheng, and for weeks he traveled about almost constantly, relating the simple events of Christ's life and the means of salvation through faith in Him.

After being delayed several weeks by a typhoon, the missionary and his family finally returned and were astonished to find nearly 1,000 Meo professing a belief in Christ!

You're fascinated by this world-class couple who look as if they belong on an Iowa farm. "Is Laos where you began working with the Meo?" you ask.

Ernie leans back in the white patio chair and smiles. Apparently you've asked the right question. For another five minutes you are again amazed at the way God works to accomplish His unchangeable purpose to reach every people in every corner of the world. Ernie tells his story:

> Another fellow and I were doing some exploratory traveling in remote Thailand in an area where these Meo or Hmong people lived. Generally the people were friendly and would readily accept us strangers into their village and give us a night of entertainment. We were handicapped because we didn't know Thai very well; my partner knew it better than I, but still he wasn't very fluent. I knew some Chinese, and the Hmong knew a little Chinese, but it was hard to communicate.
>
> We came to one village and went to the head man's house. He received us very graciously, and many people from the village came to his house to see us. Many of them, particularly the women, had never seen a white man before. They listened, but I am sure they were confused as to what we were talking about because of our broken Thai and Chinese. But we did get across a message about the God of creation and that Jesus Christ was our Savior.
>
> They let us sleep there that night, beneath the god-shelf in their home. The next morning they woke us fairly early and wanted us to follow them. Not knowing where they were going to take us, we bundled up our bedding and followed them to a new section of the village. New, good-sized homes stood amid the stumps of freshly cut jungle trees. We were taken inside one of the homes. They put out the woven bamboo mats, brought us tea, and soon crowds came and filled the room. Dzunga, the head of the home, said, "Now, tell us more about this Jesus that you were talking about. We want to know more about this person."
>
> So between the two of us we told them about Jesus the best we could throughout the day—starting in Genesis and going right on through to Revelation! They seemed to become more and more interested as our story progressed.
>
> They asked us to stay overnight. And the next night.

And the next. Finally, after a week, they told us that a group of them wanted to become Christians! This was quite unexpected since our language skills were so poor; and on a first trip it is unusual to have that kind of response. But they asked us what they needed to do, and we told them to first get rid of their spirit-worshiping articles and fetishes—to take them out of their houses and burn them.

After they accepted Jesus, they wanted to know what else they should do.

We taught them how to pray and sang a few songs with them. Then they asked how they were to live this new way, and would someone come to teach them? Would we come to live with them and teach them?

On the spot I had to make a decision. Mertie and the children—under two years of age—were too far away through the jungle to consult. I said, "Yes."

And so we began the work among the Meo or Hmong of Thailand, and the result is seen in thousands of believers in Thailand today.

But why were we so warmly received?

Months later we found out that the man, Dzunga, who had opened his home to us, had a son named Doong, who a few years earlier had almost died. The whole village had done everything they could to appease their gods, yet the boy was not healed. A broken, desperate Dzunga remembered hearing of a very powerful God, *Yesu,* from someone somewhere—possibly from a trader in Laos. The father prayed to Him: "If you are a God who has power, heal my son!"

Doong was healed!

Dzunga and the entire village were amazed at this strong Spirit, but they had no idea how to worship Him. Then, several years later, we "big-noses" came stumbling into his village proclaiming the name of *Yesu*—the eternal One, the Savior of love.

You nod at Ernie's story. "Must feel pretty good to have fit so nicely into what God was doing at the time, hmm?"

Ernie nods and Mertie smiles.

And you sit, gazing out at the glitzy city of Singapore, sipping your guava juice and thinking about how you fit into what God is doing today. Wouldn't it be a privilege to walk into a miracle? But then, you muse, with every privilege comes . . . responsibility!

———————

So far we're fairly comfortable with the basic worldview that God is blessing His people in order to bless every people group on earth with His offer of redemption. His repeated promise to Abraham, Isaac, and Jacob in Genesis is as clear as His unchangeable purpose.

But let's move on to the book of Exodus. Suddenly all our well-worn stories of baby Moses in the bullrushes, frogs and flies and rivers of blood, the parting of the Red Sea and the drowning of the Egyptians, the Ten Commandments and the wandering in the wilderness, seem to suggest that God picked out the Hebrews and virtually dropped His interest in all the other heathen nations of the earth. We may have thought that the story of the Old Testament is simply an illustrative history of the antics and foibles of the Israelites as they formed a lineage to produce the Messiah.

But think again, remembering that God's purpose in blessing all the families of the earth is unchangeable. Let's take another glimpse at the stories of the Exodus in light of His heart for all peoples.

A Kingdom of Priests

Just before giving the Ten Commandments God set Moses straight on Israel's role in His great purpose. Moses is to relay to the sons of Israel:

> "If you will indeed obey My voice and keep My covenant, then you shall be My own possession among all the peoples, for all the earth is Mine; and you shall be to Me a kingdom of priests and a holy nation" (Exodus 19:5–6).

The people were ecstatic about God's proposal and answered, "All that the LORD has spoken we will do!" (Exodus 19:8). And the rest of the chapter describes the "ordination service" the Lord performed to consecrate the Hebrews as "priests." But priests to minister on behalf of whom? Well, on behalf of everybody else!

Aaron and his sons began the priestly ministry on behalf of the children of Israel themselves; the entire tribe of the Levites then were given this responsibility as the nation grew. In the same way, the Israelites as a people were to mediate as priests for the rest of the human race—for the nations.

They learned what priests do by watching Aaron. Yes, they noticed certain privileges in serving as a priest; for example, you get direct access to God! But they also noticed that there was a job to be done. Once a year the high priest would nervously step into the Holy of Holies. Why was he nervous? Because if he had unconfessed sin in his life, God would strike him dead! The Israelites were to get the hint: Your personal pleasure might accommodate all sorts of sins, but in your role as a priest for others there is high accountability, because God's name is at stake.

Once inside the Holy of Holies, did the high priest immediately begin whining for a salary increase? New sandals for the family? An easier life? No, the priesthood is not a position that centers on privileges for the priest. Instead, it's focused on others. Inside, the priest sprinkled sacrificial blood on the Mercy Seat, interceding for others. Then as the priest came out of that time alone with God, he was to start serving the people. The priests rolled up their sleeves, carved up the sacrificed animals, and fed the people. Some of those grill-fests lasted up to three days—so there was plenty of work to be done!

The priesthood was acted out clearly: Alone with God, intercede for the people. Out among the people, serve them. Israel was to be a nation of priests, interceding for and serving the nations of the world in the name of God.

When they said, "All that the LORD has spoken we will do," did the Israelites realize what they were in for? Probably not any more than you did when you received Christ and vowed essentially the same thing. Representing God to all the people groups of the earth was quite a responsibility. They had no linguistic methodology for crossing cultural barriers, no transportation convenience, no completed Bible. But God promised that if they would simply obey Him, He would use them to bless every other people: "The people whom I formed for Myself will declare My praise" (Isaiah 43:21).

He chose them, not to bless them at the exclusion of every

other family of the earth, and not to single them out because of their superiority. Rather, He chose them to take on the responsibility of serving as priests whose parish was the entire world.

God promised that as they obeyed Him, the children of Israel would be royal priests (one rendition of "kingdom of priests") blessed with two great privileges—God's personal protection and God's holiness: "'You shall be My own possession . . . and you shall be . . . a holy nation'" (Exodus 19:5–6).

The Hebrews were not originally a people; Abraham, you recall, was simply one of an Assyrian or barbarian people group. Out of His infinite grace God formed Israel as His own people among all the other peoples. We will come to appreciate this fact as one of the most comforting truths that we as New Testament believers enjoy—being a people He has chosen to be His own possession.

God blessed Israel with His holiness. A holy nation, or people, indicates one "set apart for a particular service." God in His grace determined to set apart or sanctify this people that He formed not because of their inherent goodness or their superiority over other peoples. "The LORD did not set His love on you nor choose you because you were more in number than any of the peoples, for you were the fewest of all peoples, but because the LORD loved you and kept the oath which He swore to your forefathers" (Deuteronomy 7:7–8). The King James Version of Exodus 19:5 refers to Israel as a people "above all people." A better translation is "among all the peoples."

God's plan to bless His people and through their priestly intercession to bless all the peoples of the earth would have worked wonderfully if they had obeyed Him and kept His covenant. Their prescribed part was simple: daily, devoted obedience. God promised His chosen people, "You will be called the priests of the LORD; you will be spoken of as ministers of our God" (Isaiah 61:6) with all the privileges of a priesthood. The results?

> Instead of humiliation they [the "foreigners"] will shout for joy over their portion. Therefore they will possess a double portion in their land, everlasting joy will be theirs. . . .

And I will . . . make an everlasting covenant with them. Then their offspring will be known among the nations, and their descendants in the midst of the peoples. All who see them will recognize them because they are the offspring whom the Lord has blessed. (Isaiah 61:7–9)

The nations, the people groups, would be blessed as God's people represented Him well in their protected, holy role as priests.

What would be their priestly message? A representation of God's character, reputation, and saving grace. They were to uplift God's name.

The Name Above All Names

A name in most cultures reveals the character of the one who carries the name, and God's name is no exception. Among the dozens of names given to God to describe His character, God chooses two for the Israelites to proclaim to the nations:

- *Elohim*, a plural term suggesting His triune, supreme deity—a name speaking of His power and role as Creator
- *YHWH*, the self-existent One, the "I Am Who I Am" of Exodus 3:14. Used nearly 7,000 times in the Old Testament, this name is linked to God's holiness (Leviticus 11:44–45), His hatred of sin (Genesis 6:3–7), and His provision of salvation (Isaiah 53:1, 5–6, 10).

He uses these names as an expression of who He is to Moses:

"The LORD, the LORD God, compassionate and gracious, slow to anger, and abounding in lovingkindness and truth; who keeps lovingkindness for thousands, who forgives iniquity, transgression and sin; yet He will by no means leave the guilty unpunished, visiting the iniquity of fathers on the children and on the grandchildren to the third and fourth generations" (Exodus 34:6–7).

Segments of this catechism-like description of God's character are repeated throughout the Old Testament (see Numbers 14:18; Psalm 103:8; 145:8–21; Joel 2:13; Micah 7:18; Jonah 4:2). This description and the meanings of *YHWH* were undoubtedly coupled with what the New Testament surprisingly calls "the gospel [preached] beforehand to Abraham, saying, 'ALL THE NATIONS WILL BE BLESSED IN YOU'" (Galatians 3:8). This "Old Testament Gospel" spoke of the coming One who would crush Satan's head, by whom "God would justify the Gentiles [all non-Jewish peoples] by faith" (Galatians 3:8).

The priestly children of Israel were to proclaim the powerful, holy, redeeming character of the Lord God as they represented His name:

> "Give thanks to the LORD, call on His name. Make known His deeds among the peoples; make them remember that His name is exalted." Praise the LORD in song, for He has done excellent things; let this be known throughout the earth. (Isaiah 12:4–5) (See also Psalm 48:10; 66:4; 86:8–9; 96:1–10; 113:3–4.)

The formula could work: God's kingdom of priests would obey, and God would ensure that through them His saving grace was proclaimed as a blessing to all peoples. The perfect scenario is seen by Jeremiah. God's people as His priests would say:

> O LORD, my strength and my stronghold, and my refuge in the day of distress, to You the nations will come from the ends of the earth and say, "Our fathers have inherited nothing but falsehood, futility and things of no profit." Can man make gods for himself? Yet they are not gods! "Therefore behold, I am going to make them know . . . My power and My might; and they shall know that My name is [*YHWH*] the LORD" (Jeremiah 16:19–21).

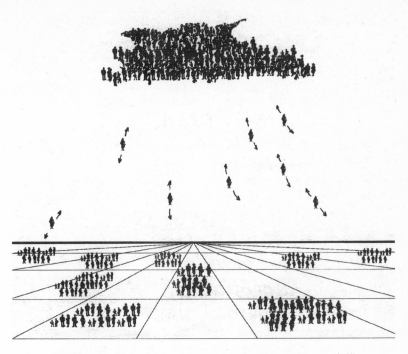

"I will say to those who were not my people, 'You are My people!'"
(Hosea 2:23; Romans 9:25).

The Message

Imagine the reaction of today's public to the interviews and incidents of the Exodus of the children of Israel; focal in the news stories would be the reputation of the God of the Hebrews:

> Headline in the *Pyramid Pilot*: Hebrew Rebel Threatens Hail Next! The story: At daybreak Cairo time the renegade Hebrew Moses insisted on an audience with the Pharaoh. Apparently Pharaoh had been sleepless through the night with boils—as reported throughout Egypt. This Moses was quoted as saying, "Thus says *YHWH*, the *Elohim* of the Hebrews. . . . 'This time I will send all My plagues on you . . . so that you may know that there is no one like Me in all the earth. . . . For this cause I have allowed you to remain, in order to show you My power and in order to proclaim My name through all the earth.'"

What will it be this time? Blood, frogs, lice, flies, killing off the livestock, and boils—what else can this *YHWH-Elohim* hit us with to get the Pharaoh's attention? Rumor is that hail is the next stage in his promotional scheme.

The trade routes are packed with foreigners fleeing from Egypt with the stories of these plagues. Estimates are that within three months every inn along the caravan roads from Europe to India, China to southern Africa, will have heard of the humiliation of Pharaoh and the Egyptian gods. Many top cabinet posts are urging negotiations with Moses for fear of what this *YHWH* might devise as His next terrorist tactic. Unnamed sources said one of the Pharaoh's servants has admitted "fearing the word of *Elohim*" and is currently bringing his servants and livestock in from the field. . . .

The news of this God-who-is-not-to-be-toyed-with spreads far and wide throughout the events of the Exodus: God divided "the water before them to make for Himself an everlasting name. . . . So You led Your people, to make for Yourself a glorious name" (Isaiah 63:12, 14 NKJV).

God used His people regardless of their understanding of His purpose: "Our fathers in Egypt did not understand Your wonders . . . but rebelled by the sea; the Red Sea. Nevertheless He saved them for His name's sake, that He might make His mighty power known" (Psalm 106:7–8 NKJV).

The eminence of His name was the leverage Moses used to "convince" God not to destroy the golden-calf-worshiping Israelites: "Why should the Egyptians speak, saying, 'With evil intent He brought them out to kill them in the mountains and to destroy them from the face of the earth'?" (Exodus 32:12). If God had brought the Israelites through such miraculous events only to blast them into oblivion in the desert, who would want to follow Him? Imagine the Egyptians who responded in reverential fear to the God of the Hebrews, whom they learned was compassionate and gracious, yet would not leave the guilty unpunished who suddenly reverted to the gods of Egypt. These old familiar gods might have been humiliated by this *YHWH-Elohim*, but at least they didn't trick their followers into following them into annihilation!

It's one of the basic themes of the Old Testament's stories of settling into the Promised Land: The name of the Lord is to be acknowledged by all peoples. When the wilderness-wandering generation of mumblers had died off, the new generation of the children of Israel crossed over the Jordan River on dry ground. Joshua later explained to the people, "The LORD your God dried up the waters of the Jordan before you . . . that all the peoples of the earth may know that the hand of the LORD is mighty" (Joshua 4:23–24).

In Jericho, the prostitute Rahab explains why she has protected the Israelite spies:

> "For we have heard how the LORD [*YHWH*, the holy Redeemer] dried up the water of the Red Sea before you when you came out of Egypt, and what you did to the two kings of the Amorites. . . . When we heard it, our hearts melted and no courage remained in any man any longer because of you; for the LORD [*YHWH*] your God [*Elohim*, the strong Creator], He is God in heaven above and on earth beneath" (Joshua 2:10–11).

Rahab's knowledge of who God is came only through traders' stories of the experiences of the Israelites; yet from this revelation of His name, she believed, obeyed, and was justified (Hebrews 11:31; James 2:25).

When the men of Ai first defeated the sons of Israel, Joshua complained, "'O LORD, what can I say since Israel has turned their back before their enemies? For the Canaanites and all the inhabitants of the land will hear of it. . . . And what will You do for Your great name?'" (Joshua 7:8–9).

Envoys from the Gibeonites told Joshua, "'Your servants have come from a very far country because of the fame of the LORD your God; for we have heard the report of Him and all that He did in Egypt'" (Joshua 9:9).

God's Unchangeable Purpose

Why did God perform incredible miracles to free Israel from slavery in Egypt and lead them through the wilderness to a land flowing with milk and honey?

Our usual answer has something to do with their being His *chosen* people. But chosen for what? Chosen to be blessed, while all the other people groups of the world suffer as captives to Satan's dominion of darkness? Chosen and specially treated, like spoiled children, their disobediences tolerated until they finally produce a Messiah? Or chosen as a kingdom of priests to perform the responsibilities of God's purpose—to offer redemptive blessing to all the peoples of the earth? To be used as set apart vessels to demonstrate God's character, His name, to all the nations?

Spend some time rethinking many of your favorite stories from Exodus, Numbers, Joshua, and Judges. How did God use each incident to further His eternal unchangeable purpose to bless His people and through them bless every people?

The Priesthood of the Believers

Let's bring this chapter's input a little closer to home. Why has God chosen *me*? Why has He left me on the earth, instead of whisking me off to the joyous ease of heaven the instant I received Christ? To live a blessed life while millions from unreached people groups suffer under Satan's dominion of darkness? To be specially treated like a spoiled child, my disobediences tolerated until I finally die to live in Christlikeness eternally? Or have I been chosen as one in a kingdom of priests to perform the responsibilities of God's purpose—to offer redemptive blessing to all the peoples of the earth—my own people included? To be used as a set apart vessel to demonstrate God's character, His name, to all the nations?

What if I were to spend some quality time rethinking some of my favorite experiences? How can God use an incident I went through to sharpen my message of His character, to further His unchangeable purpose?

The wonderful privilege and the crucial responsibility of the priesthood are repeated in the New Testament. If you are a believer you are one of "A CHOSEN RACE, A royal PRIESTHOOD, A HOLY NATION, A PEOPLE FOR God's OWN POSSESSION" (1 Peter 2:9). The blessings listed are obvious, and teaching on the "priesthood of the believer" often is relegated to the privileged access we each have into the very throne room of God.

But the verse continues with our New Testament responsibility: "That you may proclaim the excellencies of Him who has called you out of darkness into His marvelous light."

This passage, like the Old Testament passage it parallels, isn't only about you as an individual. It's about you as one of the people of God. Think of it. You're not foremost a Jew or Gentile—Germanic or Arabic or Korean or Kurdish or Meo or Singaporean. You're foremost a member of a new people group that's drawn one person at a time from the peoples of the earth: "You once were NOT A PEOPLE, but now you are THE PEOPLE OF GOD" (1 Peter 2:10). We're in this together, across all kinds of cultural boundaries.

The priesthood of the believer—more accurately, of believers—is not just for our own benefit. Our priesthood is about being blessed in order to bless the nations—to intercede for and to serve the nations. Our own nation included!

Best of all, as we fulfill our role as a nation of priests, we're serving God:

> To him who loves us and has freed us from our sins by his blood, and has made us to be a kingdom and priests to serve his God and Father—to him be glory and power for ever and ever! Amen. (Revelation 1:5–6 NIV)

For Further Thought

1. Study and meditate on 1 Peter 2:9–10 to clarify your personal and your church's standing as a *kingdom of priests*.
2. Pray daily during the coming month for direction on how you can be a holy and effective "priest" on behalf of one of the people groups listed in chapter 2. Find out whatever you can—which may be very little—to guide you in that first step of interceding for this people. God, who has that people listed in His Register of the Peoples (Psalm 87:6) knows intimately whom you're praying for!
3. Once you've done some homework on a people, share your insights with at least one friend and ask her or him to pray for that ethnic group as well.

CHAPTER 7

THE BEST OF TIMES, THE WORST OF TIMES:

Solomon's One Shining Moment

Calcutta. After a week in the city you are desensitized a bit to the swirl of smells and sights of poverty, the 12 million people around you, the half million who live on the streets. You're bouncing along on a city bus trying to finish a dog-eared paperback about Gandhi, and you're still upset from an early entry in the biography. When Gandhi was asked about the authenticity of the Gospel, he replied that he rejected Christianity because of what he saw—and didn't see—in the character of Christians.

But what if Hindus could see the character of *Elohim*, the

Deity of power—of *YHWH*, the God who is a personal Redeemer, a holy Savior! You remember a recent survey report you read: 25% of the Hindus in India would consider becoming Christians if they could do it without losing their cultural and family ties, without becoming, in effect, a Westerner.

There is hope, you know. Individuals are fighting for the cause of Christ in Calcutta. A young man named Sujo John, a native of Calcutta, was in New York City and survived the 9/11 attack on the World Trade Center Towers. He and his pregnant wife travel together sharing their riveting testimonies of God's protection during the attack; amazingly, they have seen more than 30,000 people come to Christ across the world since then. Sujo returns to Calcutta periodically with short-term teams to help build a fence around a school, to minister to orphans, and to preach the Word. Individuals—like the legendary Mother Teresa—have made and are making a difference.

Across India as a whole, tens of thousands are coming to Christ. For example, among the *dalits,* the untouchables that comprise 20% of the population in hundreds of ethnic groups, the gospel is spreading exponentially. The *dalits* are not part of the caste system, and sometimes their openness to the freedom and dignity of the gospel is as much a revolt against the insults of the castes as it is a turning to Jesus. Whatever the individual motivation, Jesus Christ is building His church among the *dalits.*

The DAWN Movement (Discipling a Whole Nation) reports that a network of thirty-two ministries with 2,616 house churches grew to 8,784 churches during 2002—a growth of 336% in 12 months! Another report in a similar situation records the starting of 30,000 house churches among various *dalit* people groups in 2003 alone. During the last five years close to 1,000 grassroots church-planters have been raised up in the north Indian state of Bihar, known in years past as the "graveyard of missions." Gospel for Asia, only one of the thousands of powerful ministries in India, reports that its 14,000 local church-planters see an average of 10 new fellowships of new believers spring up *every day*!

Even among the 12% Muslim population of India, God is moving in unprecedented ways. Operation Agape reports that 800 Muslims in northern India recently became Christians.

More than 100 house churches were planted in various districts of Uttar Pradesh State in the first six months of 2004, every member a former Muslim. In West Bengal State, 15 Islamic priests and their families have been baptized as believers in Christ, and there is a growing church-planting movement among the region's Muslims.

The *World Christian Encyclopedia* lists the top three most responsive unreached peoples in the world as the Khandeshi, the Awadhi (Baiswari, Bagheli), and the Magadhi Bihari (Maghori)—all in India. With more than one billion in population—surpassing China in 2015 as the world's most populous country—India has officially insisted since 1947 that Christians comprise just 2.5% of the population. Most India-watchers suggest it's actually closer to 4%; some have suggested it's as high as 10%. Even at 4%, that's 40 million Christians in India!

But the amazing numbers that represent India aren't entirely on the side of victories for the kingdom of Christ. With—depending on your parameters for defining a "people group"—as many as 2,329 people groups, or *jathi,* speaking more than 1,652 languages, "blessing the nations" in India is complex. Visas for foreign missionaries were outlawed in 1975, and the few foreign missionaries that remain are prohibited from evangelizing. Indigenous ministries with tens of thousands of workers are moving out across the cultural boundaries within India, yet few are going to the two-thirds of the population who are in the caste systems. The personal poverty and social pain of millions in India is overwhelming. For example, more than 1.2 million children and adolescents are illegally involved in prostitution in India.

You rest the Gandhi biography in your lap and gaze blankly out the dusty bus window at the milling crowds along a main street lined with sophisticated office buildings. There's an old blind beggar being whisked away from the doors of the opulent Oberoi Grand Hotel. You hear the constant clanging of cymbals as sacrifices are made to Kali, Calcutta's namesake, the goddess of death and destruction. But she is, after all, only one of the 33 million gods worshiped in India. You see those who sit "in darkness and in the shadow of death" (Psalm 107:10) living "under the power of the devil" (Acts 10:38 NIV) all along the roadway;

you know that biblical *darkness* is not so much the absence of light but the palpable presence of evil.

You remember the tales of Ghasi Das and the remarkable Satnamis, worshipers of the true God.

It was 1817. "Throw out your idols! Worship only the true God! Quit eating meat—it lowers you in the eyes of all Hindus. Dress in white. Live simply. Wait for the coming of a red-faced man with a big hat on his head and a big book in his hand. Do what he tells you!"

This was the message the peasant Ghasi Das shouted across the flat fields of the great plain in the southeast corner of Madhya Pradesh. Of the low-caste Chamar people, Ghasi Das walked nearly 400 miles east on a pilgrimage to this very city—Calcutta. At the holy Ganges River, Ghasi Das followed the riverbank to the mouth where he came upon a red-faced man with a big hat on his head and a huge book. William Carey, the "father of modern missions," was preaching on God's heart for the peoples of India. Carey had initiated the first mission agency when the leadership of his church told him, "Young man, if God wants to evangelize the heathen, He can certainly do it without our help!"

But God was now doing it with William Carey's "help." And Ghasi Das listened intently to this foreigner's words being spoken in twisted Hindi.

Ghasi immediately set out with his message for the Chamars: "Throw out your idols! Worship the true God!" It was a call to become a new people with a new, true God; and the message found immediate widespread acceptance.

The Chamars asked, "What is the name of the true God whom you proclaim?"

"I don't know," the peasant replied, "but His name is the true name." In Hindi, "true" is *sat* and "name" is *nam*. Thus the Chamars changed their name; they became the *Satnamis*.

The Satnamis tossed out their idols and waited for the red-faced man with the big book to tell them more.

The red-faced man never came. But other foreigners did—foreigners who virtually told the True-Namers that if they would become Westernized they could meet the true God.

You suddenly realize you're nodding off in the Calcutta bus. You slap yourself awake and look at the faces on the sidewalks in the dusty sunlight. You're suddenly glad you don't know everything; you're glad you're not God. Imagine knowing the hearts of every one of these millions giving themselves to the domain of the goddess of death, of the billions worldwide. Imagine knowing the despair of those seeking the True Name, of those disappointed by some of the missionaries of the past whose idea of blessing the nations was converting them to Western culture. Imagine the heart of God breaking for the 55,000 people who die daily here in India and around the world without ever hearing the True Name.

For the first time in your around-the-world journey you slump breathless in your seat as you're hit with despair.

The Ups and Downs

Moses made God's covenant perfectly clear to the sons of Israel: "If you diligently obey the LORD your God . . . all the peoples of the earth shall see that you are called by the name of the LORD . . . and the LORD will make you abound" (Deuteronomy 28:1, 10–11). A rough paraphrase might be: *If you live rightly, all the world's unreached peoples will recognize that you as God's people bear the wonderful character of God, and as a result, the people of God will grow with new believers.*

Before Joshua died at the ripe old age of 110, he reminded Israel to serve the Lord and to consider the dire consequences of disobedience. Their response? "Far be it from us that we should forsake the LORD to serve other gods; for the LORD our God is He who . . . preserved us . . . among all the peoples through whose midst we passed" (Joshua 24:16–17).

But we all know the story: God soon had to reprimand the sons of Israel with "You have not obeyed Me" (Judges 2:2). They refused to drive out the inhabitants of the Promised Land; instead, they intermarried and began to worship other gods.

Incidentally, why did God give such drastic orders as: "You shall not leave alive anything that breathes. But you shall utterly destroy them" (Deuteronomy 20:16–17)? Because God knew "their detestable things which they have done for their gods"

(20:18) (sexually focused religious practices) would infect and destroy the Israelites as a people. The modern-day AIDS epidemic across the continent of Africa threatens the very existence of whole people groups. Israel would have undergone pestilence, consumption, fever, inflammation, boils, tumors, scabs, and itch from which they could not be healed—leading to madness, blindness, and bewilderment of heart—until they would destroy themselves (See Deuteronomy 28:19–45).

Second, God allowed the total destruction of people groups such as the Hittites, Amorites, Perizzites, Hivites, Jebusites, and Canaanites because He knew they would never as a people turn to Him. That is, the Hittites as a people would never repent even though some individual Hittites such as Uriah (2 Samuel 11) would respond to God's call and stand before the throne of the Lamb (Revelation 5:9). This parallels what God can do in an individual life: God in His perfect foreknowledge knows the point after which a person will never repent, when he or she will simply continue destroying his or her life and the lives of others. God may at that point actually allow the person's death. (Study through the sobering factor of the "sin unto death" even among believers in 1 John 5:16–17.) God in His infinite wisdom knows when the final judgment of a people group is inevitable, when they will experience nothing but the disease, the suffering, and the futility of their bondage to darkness. Make no mistake, the fearsome God of the Old Testament and the God of the twenty-first century does allow the destruction of people who refuse to respond to the light He has given them—whether it is the initial light of creation, conscience, and instinct, or the further light of the Gospel as revealed in Scripture. (See Psalm 19:1–4; Romans 1:18–23.)

Because of the Israelites' disobedience, the death of Joshua was followed by nearly 400 years of roller-coaster ups and downs as God's kingdom of priests discredited His name, then repented under a God-appointed leader, then discredited God's name, then repented under a God-appointed leader, then. . . . (See Samuel's recap of these events in 1 Samuel 12:8–12.)

The Ups

Three—and only three—kings ruled a united Israel: Saul, David, and Solomon. Samuel appointed Saul as the first king even while scolding the nation for their rejection of the Lord God as their king: "Your wickedness is great which you have done in the sight of the Lord by asking for yourselves a king" (1 Samuel 12:17). But Samuel also warned them not to turn aside from following the Lord, "for the Lord will not abandon His people on account of His great name" (12:22). Yet Saul proved unworthy to lead a nation whose God was the Lord.

David's exploits in the name of the Lord are some of the most familiar stories of the Old Testament. He shouted to the Philistine Goliath, "You come to me with a sword, a spear, and a javelin, but I come to you in the name of the Lord of hosts, the God of the armies of Israel, whom you have taunted. This day the Lord will deliver you up into my hands . . . that all the earth may know that there is a God in Israel" (1 Samuel 17:45–46).

And David is probably the one who penned or commissioned such verses as "God blesses us, that all the ends of the earth may fear Him" (Psalm 67:7). The faithful Israelites of David's time sang that line over and over again. Perhaps David's constant reference in his psalms to "the peoples," "the nations," and "the ends of the earth" suggest why he became "a man after God's own heart"—the heart that yearns after the world's lost.

And Israel's role as a shining light to all the peoples of the earth was probably never as prominent as during the early reign of David's son Solomon. The Israelite of Solomon's glory days would say, "Of course, God blesses us to be a blessing to the nations." Hadn't they all been at the temple dedication ceremonies and memorized Solomon's dedicatory prayer?

> Concerning the foreigner who . . . comes from a far country for Your name's sake (for they will hear of Your great name and Your mighty hand, and of Your outstretched arm); when he comes and prays toward this house, hear in heaven . . . and do according to all for which the foreigner calls to You, in order that all the peoples of the earth may know Your name, to fear You, as do Your people Israel, and that they may know that this house which I have built is called by Your name. (1 Kings 8:41–43)

Every time the Israelites came into the silver-decked and

gold-covered temple consecrated by the very heart of God (1 Kings 9:3), they entered through what became known in later days as "The Court of the Gentiles." In the days of Isaiah God confirmed the international scope of His blessing on this temple: "Also the foreigners who join themselves to the Lord . . . I will bring to My holy mountain and make them joyful in My house of prayer. . . . For My house will be called a house of prayer for all the peoples" (Isaiah 56:6–7). (Is it any wonder Jesus drove out the money changers and peddlers from the Court of the Gentiles, shouting this reference? (See Mark 11:15–17.)

Even those from the outlying countryside of Israel were reminded that Israel's blessing had to do with the uplifting of God's name among the nations when the Queen of Sheba came to town. The trade routes from China to India to southern Africa to Spain buzzed with the news: This ruler of the Sabeans in the southern region of Arabia traveled on camelback for 1,200 miles to meet Solomon. She brought him about $50,000 in gold, and "a very great amount of spices and precious stones" (1 Kings 10:10).

The obvious question was asked and answered all along the routes: Why did she come? Because "when the queen of Sheba heard about the fame of Solomon concerning the name of the LORD, she came to test him with difficult questions" (1 Kings 10:1). The name of the Lord—the personal Redeemer, the holy, eternal One, the all-powerful Creator, the God of Solomon—provoked her quest.

Apparently Solomon answered all her "difficult questions" concerning the name of the Lord and His blessing. "'It was a true report,'" she said, "'which I heard in my own land. . . . How blessed are your men, how blessed are these your servants. . . . Blessed be the LORD your God'" (1 Kings 10:6–9).

God was accomplishing His unchangeable purpose of blessing His people to be a blessing to all peoples. Then Solomon fell in love.

The Downs

Imagine. Solomon marries the daughter of the pharaoh of Egypt. He marries a Moabitess and an Ammonite; both of these people groups were the descendants of Lot's daughters' incest, and both were overt rebels against the Lord God of Abraham. Solomon also marries an Edomite woman, a Sidonian, and a Hittite woman. And another Hittite woman. And another. Can you imagine 700 wedding ceremonies? And keeping track of 300 mistresses besides?

Obviously the potential for Solomon's marital problems was great; he loved and married a few too many hundreds of women. And the potential for spiritual danger increased with each new wife. God had expressly commanded the Israelites not to inter-marry with other peoples because "they will surely turn your heart away after their gods" (1 Kings 11:2).

And that is exactly what happened. As Solomon gave in to the pleading of his wives to be able to worship their own gods, his own "heart was not wholly devoted to the LORD his God, as the heart of David his father had been. For Solomon went after Ashtoreth the goddess of the Sidonians and after Milcom the detestable idol of the Ammonites. . . . Then Solomon built a high place for Chemosh the detestable idol of Moab, on the mountain which is east of Jerusalem, and for Molech the detest-able idol of the sons of Ammon. Thus also he did for all his foreign wives, who burned incense and sacrificed to their gods" (1 Kings 11:4, 7–8).

More is at stake here, of course, than Solomon's personal spiritual welfare. Even more is on the line than his poor perform-ance as a role model for his own people. The name, the charac-ter, of the Lord is being blasphemed. And the news spreads quickly.

Solomon has a household full of 700 "foreign correspon-dents" who pass on news regularly to their royal families, their friends, and their own people groups. Imagine Solomon's wives listening for their homeland dialects in the marketplace, catching up on home-front news from travelers and traders coming through Jerusalem, the world trade route center.

And what news do they pass on? Great news for the home-land! "Solomon is now worshiping our god! Our gods are back in vogue!" And as the traders caravan out of Jerusalem, the news is validated. High on the mountain east of Jerusalem are temples to Milcom, Molech, Ashtoreth, and other gods.

God's reputation is being destroyed.

The Never-Ending Story

You may have felt this yourself: You're not ashamed of God since you know Him to be wonderful. But you're sometimes ashamed to be associated with His people. The very humans who are given the responsibility of representing His character—His name—are sometimes jerks. Or bigots. Or cruel crusaders. Or hypocrites. Or more immoral than nonbelievers.

God is jealous about His name, about His reputation, because a bad reputation drives people away. And His plan is to "draw all men to Himself"! "'Now therefore, what do I have here,' declares the LORD, 'seeing that My people have been taken away without cause? . . . Those who rule over them howl, and My name is continually blasphemed all day long'" (Isaiah 52:5). One thousand years later the apostle Paul complained to God's people, "THE NAME OF GOD IS BLASPHEMED AMONG THE GENTILES [the peoples] BECAUSE OF YOU" (Romans 2:24).

One thousand years after that the marauding Crusaders slaughtered the "infidel" Muslim men, women, and children of the Mediterranean in the name of Christ, and Islam has never forgotten the atrocities of these "Christians."

Nearly 1,000 years after the Crusades Mahatma Gandhi in India says he rejects Christ's Gospel because of the demeanor of those who call themselves His people.

And in Emakhandeni, Zimbabwe, a husky man dips a wad of snuff, a ritual of ancestral spirit worship, and tells his two young Christian visitors, "This Jesus and this Bible is from white men to cool down Africans so whites can rule over them and tax them and steal their land. You young people swallow many things without chewing them. This Jesus is the ancestral spirit for whites, but we Africans have nothing to do with Him. We have our own ancestors."

Frank Mayis and Lifa Ndlovu, on one of their first evangelistic visits, aren't quite sure how to respond. "Do you pray to God?" Lifa asks.

"You're too young to know anything!" the man says. "I can't

pray to God directly. He's too great. I have to speak to the spirits of my ancestors and ask them to speak to God for me because they're closer to Him. God is too great! This Jesus is just a white man!"

Now thousands of miles northeast of Zimbabwe, across the Indian Ocean, you step down from the bus and trip over chunks of broken concrete in the debris of a Calcutta street. And you wonder how you've been doing as a priest, a representative of the character of God.

You round a corner to a dirt lane of sour-smelling market stalls and weave through milling shoppers in dusty white. You pass under strands of flax and tapestries; flies persistently cling to your shirt. Within the block you count four video stalls—booths with a television and videocassette recorder or DVD player with intent audiences of two or three. You hear the familiar, goofy chicken theme of the old *Benny Hill* comedy show of the '80s. You slump against a post and watch a corner of the screen at one stall showing *Sex in the City*. Another blares music videos under a sign in English: "Risky Music Video!"

Store after store offers English cigarettes and German tabloids. And you glimpse in several dark, back-row stalls the brassy colors of porno magazines from the West. You feel the gritty darkness of satanic oppression over this city like a net over your shoulders.

And you find yourself getting angry. Because you know that imperialism, materialism, and sexual obsession is what much of the spiritually blinded unreached world thinks of as "Christian." Because of the reputation of "Christianized" countries, the name of God is often blasphemed among the world's peoples.

You know that any nation that claims to be God's people and that discredits His name is in for trouble. "Taking God's name in vain" doesn't mean swearing so much as dragging His character—His deity, power, redemption, and holiness—through the mud. And the realization scares you as you remember a dire rant from the prophet Ezekiel:

> I chose Israel . . . to bring them out from the land of Egypt into a land that I had selected for them . . . but they rebelled against Me. Then I resolved to pour out my wrath

on them . . . but I acted for the sake of My name, that it should not be profaned in the sight of the nations. . . .

And I gave them My statutes . . . but the house of Israel rebelled against Me in the wilderness. . . . Then I resolved to pour out My wrath on them . . . but I acted for the sake of My name, that it should not be profaned in the sight of the nations. . . .

I said to their children in the wilderness, "Do not walk in the statutes of your fathers. . . ." But the children rebelled against Me. . . . So I resolved to pour out My wrath on them. . . . But I withdrew My hand and acted for the sake of My name, that it should not be profaned in the sight of the nations. (Ezekiel 20:5–6, 8–9, 18, 21–22)

The ups and downs are obvious. Mostly the downs. Israel was fast becoming like any other people group: " 'We will be like the nations, like the tribes of the lands, serving wood and stone' " (Ezekiel 20:32). But God would persevere in His great plan to reach every people. In spite of their evil intentions, He says, " 'I will prove Myself holy among you in the sight of the nations. . . . Then you will know that I am the Lord when I have dealt with you for My name's sake' " (Ezekiel 20:41, 44).

Today God's reputation among the peoples of the earth is at stake every time His people go after other "gods," every time they blaspheme His name among the nations. The Old Testament warnings that God resolves to pour out His wrath makes you uncomfortable—especially if your passport country is one of those with a fine Christianized motto such as "In God we trust."

For Further Thought

1. Read through Isaiah 56:6–7 and Mark 11:15–17. When was the last time you heard a message on the fact that Jesus' indignation in this very familiar New Testament story was at least in part due to Israel's selfishness in not allowing the Gentiles—the "nations"—to worship at the temple? What does this suggest about our own selfishness in concentrating so much on top-line interpretations of Scripture that we rarely mention the bottom line of God's heart for every people group?

2. Get out your world map or globe and pinpoint Calcutta and Zimbabwe. How is the reputation of the Lord—His name that speaks of deity and personal redemption—treated in these locations today?

3. Pray for the dozens of various people groups clustered in Calcutta. The futility of trying to feed every malnourished street orphan, or of teaching job skills to every homeless youth, can keep us from praying realistically about such depressing situations and groups of humanity. But aren't we angry at such injustice—that Satan keeps these hundreds of thousands captive in his evil domain?

   Our anger at injustice can keep us crying out to God for Calcutta. He promises that "blessed is the people group whose God is the Lord." If we pray against the strongholds of Satan over this city, if we petition God to thrust forth hundreds of church-planting teams into Calcutta, as people group after people group make the Lord their God, Satan's control will be broken. Jesus Christ says to the hopeless, desperate people of the world's mega-cities that He has come "'To preach the Gospel to the poor . . . to proclaim release to the captives, and recovery of sight to the blind, to set free those who are downtrodden, to proclaim the favorable year of the Lord'" (Luke 4:18–19). The babies and young people and the aged of Calcutta will have a chance to enjoy the blessing of God! Pray for Calcutta.

4. Review the information in chapter 3 regarding the interlink of the spiritual and natural worlds. Jot down some of the details you've learned in this chapter about Calcutta, and share your concerns for serious prayer for that great city with several friends.

CHAPTER 8

PURSES WITH HOLES:

God's Purpose the Hard Way

Somewhere in Western Sahara. Okay, so you feel like an idiot—you have no earthly idea where you are. You casually ask Robert, the Brit who organized this trip and is driving your big Toyota Land Cruiser. He sticks out his lip, looks at the flat dirt—sand to the horizon—and says, "Haven't a clue."

The other white Land Cruiser broke a condenser belt around noon. No air-conditioning. And now, around six in the evening, it's 114° F outside. Api, the Berber guide with the piercing green eyes, drives that other airless vehicle while the eight of your team are squeezed into Robert's air-conditioned Cruiser. Both vehicles are doing maybe 60 miles per hour, side by side, floating rooster tails of dust rising behind you in the slanting sun. And Robert doesn't have a clue.

One of your squished seatmates yells to Robert, "I thought we were following the barrels!"

The French nearly 100 years ago positioned a line of weighted 50-gallon drums on this north-south route across the Sahara, each exactly as far as the horizon from the previous barrel—usually five miles apart.

"We were." He keeps the pedal to the metal, and your side-by-side SUVs race alone across the vast desert that now becomes low, rolling dunes of sand. Lost.

From your orientation sessions before this bizarre trek from the Mediterranean to Cote d'Ivoire, you know it will be dark in approximately two hours. Lost is one thing. Lost in the dark—without a safe area to camp—is another. You keep thinking of the two groups of tourists who'd been taken hostage in the past couple of years. Algerian and Western Saharan rebels had tried to bargain their demands by threatening to hand over the tourist hostages in body bags. And you're not even tourists! You've been distributing *Jesus* film videos at every settlement along your route, and driving directly south across Mauritania and a leg of Senegal seemed a perfectly reasonable, adventurous way to continue the distribution ministry in Cote d'Ivoire. At least it had seemed reasonable at the time.

Api, the Berber driver, honks and motions for us to stop. Robert slows gradually, allowing the dust to settle before he comes to a full stop. He climbs out, walks over to the other Land Cruiser window, and talks to the guide. He's back in a minute.

"Well, everybody, we really don't know where we are. Api's GPS unit conked out a couple of hours ago in the heat. I thought he knew where he was going, and he thought I knew where I was going. But neither of us has seen a barrel in, oh, maybe sixty miles."

You're not sure how to respond. You know how you would if this weren't a mission trip!

Robert says, "The best bet is to stop now and set up camp. If we turn around and try to follow our tracks back it'll soon be too dark. And there's no good reason to keep driving ahead till dark and waste fuel since we don't know where we are. So, sorry, we'll have to switch off the vehicle. No more air-conditioning. And it won't be dark for a couple hours. So, uh, I guess we'll just sweat a lot. Everybody out."

It's about an hour later, sitting in the shade of a green tarp stretched between the Cruisers, that you begin to realize how serious being lost in the Sahara is. There's the matter of enough fuel. Water. Any mechanical breakdown here where no other vehicle would travel. And to backtrack till you sight a barrel isn't a good idea either. After dark the eerie wind will gust as it does every night and probably erase your vehicles' tracks. Robert keeps using a word you've come to loathe: *dicey*.

The air is still so hot that you don't actually sweat; any perspiration instantly evaporates, actually leaving you feeling chilled. But you know your body temp is way up there. This is not good. You gulp water periodically, even as all of you pray and pray. Api watches.

The sun does finally go down, and the sky finally darkens. Robert suddenly squints toward the horizon. You all look.

A figure is walking toward you through the gathering twilight. A man. No, a little boy in a flapping blue *jellaba*. He's striding purposefully, as if he's power-walking in a workout.

You all stand; then, pushing on hats, you walk out toward him. It takes maybe five minutes of wading through the sand to meet. You all smile, act animated, and kneel to get on his level. He seems very composed, doesn't seem to be dehydrated or lost. Or even worried.

But no one can understand him. Not even Api. "He is Tuareg, I think."

Robert looks east, in the dark direction where the boy had come from. "Well, let's get him back to the trucks."

Once seated, the boy takes a great guzzle of water, talks and talks, pointing to the direction from which he came. You're all dumbfounded. There is absolutely no settlement, no well, no report of any nomadic herders in any of the southwestern Sahara. You all talk at once. Api tries to find a few words common to Tuareg and Arabic. Team members chatter about the predicament and the amazing appearance of this boy.

Robert settles in his canvas camp chair and tells you about the Tuareg. "They were probably present at the Day of Pentecost in Jerusalem. It was about mid-first century that the Tuareg became known as a Christian people, living all along the North African coast. Their men wear those distinctive indigo-blue *jellaba* robes. And every warrior has over his shoulder a leather sash, sometimes as a bandelero for bullets, and guess what's carved in the leather?"

"No clue," you say.

"A cross. If you ask why there is a cross on every man's sash, they can't tell you. Tradition, they say. In the 600s Islamic invaders pushed the Christian Tuareg south into the desert. The Sahara wasn't as vast then, and the Tuareg as a huge tribe emerged on the south edge of it—in Mauritania, Senegal, Niger. But Islamic militants were there, too, forcing people to become Muslims. At that point, the Tuareg were too weakened to resist, and they gave up their Christian heritage and became Muslim. And—"

Api interrupts. "I think, Mr. Robert, we should drive where he is pointing."

"Tonight? In the dark?"

Api nods. His green eyes say what we all know: He's been constantly warning us not to travel at night in the Sahara. "We should go now."

You're thinking as you pack up camp and climb back into the vehicles, *Get out of your comfort zone. Find the edge of adventure. The edge of faith.* At least that's what the short-term missions brochure had said.

An hour later the boy has guided Api and your two vehicles slowly across nearly eight miles of sand dunes, rocky crevices, and dirt mounds. You're in the first vehicle as you nose up at the top of a dune, then tilt forward and down into a small sand valley. You see the light of a fire. Next to two desert trucks. With people milling around.

The boy's parents alternate between hugging him, looking in wonder at your foreign faces, whapping the boy's head, and then hugging him again.

You set up your own camp next to this Tuareg family's camp, which has as its centerpiece a big red 50-gallon drum. And you hear the story from Api after he's talked around the fire in Arabic to the parents: About six o'clock that evening the boy had become uncontrollable in the truck, demanding to be let out. They thought he was going to be sick, and watched him run up a dune and disappear over the top. Both trucks stopped, and the big family decided to set up camp for the night even though it was earlier than normal. And maybe half an hour later the parents realized the boy had never come back. By the time they too had run to the top of the dune, he was nowhere to be seen, tracks obliterated by the rising winds. They had been beside themselves with fear. And thanked Api over and over for bringing the boy back. When they asked the boy why he ran away, he basically told them, "I had to."

Months later you get an e-mail from Robert in England:

> I just spoke about our distribution ministry at a church in Harpendon. I asked if there were any questions, and an old fellow who was on a prayer committee for our trip asked, "What about the boy?" I said dumbly, "The boy?" Then he told of the day he and two others were praying for us, and it seemed God was telling them to pray for a boy. They didn't know if a boy was ill, or was responding to the Gospel, or what, but they prayed! And I told him!
>
> Remember to pray for the Tuareg, that great people who lost their inheritance as a people in Jesus Christ and have now become one of the world's most resistant unreached nations.
> Best Regards, Robert

Losing the Blessing

Can you imagine being part of a culture like the Tuareg, a people who decide to no longer believe "Blessed is the nation whose God is the Lord"?

Frankly, you don't like to think about the possibility of God removing His blessing from your own culture. After trekking through the Sahara (Yes, in the true story the group made it to Cote d'Ivoire—seeing even more God-adventures on the way!) you couldn't wait to get home—home to clean, even streets, plenty of fresh food in sparkling grocery stores, cool water, and shade. You wanted to be home with logical people and the normality of life in your society that has been so deeply influenced by godly values. But is your tidy, familiar nation considering reversing its allegiance to God?

What is God saying to Christianized people groups in the quickening pace as He completes His historic, unchangeable plan?

The warnings your culture has endured about sliding into moral depravity, doing drugs, ignoring church affiliation, all seem—admit it—exaggerated, and therefore a bit ineffective. After all, there are and have been plenty of worse cultures. Even from what you've learned in your global journey so far, more evil activity has gone on for centuries in other nations.

Is your nation so pervasively evil that it's headed for hell? Of course you can find evil here and there among individuals. But when you've staggered through the atmosphere of spiritual oppression in cities like Calcutta, the worst of Sydney or San Francisco or Liverpool seems like a Sunday school picnic by comparison. The older generation has always complained that the younger generation is disgustingly loose, uneducated, off-track, and immorally going to the dogs. Is your country actually in trouble because of all the sins she commits?

Or does judgment loom because of what she omits?

"To whom much is given . . . much will be required" (Luke 12:48 NKJV). You know that your people in your country have been given much.

Has your nation claimed to belong to God and yet gone after other gods, defaming God's name? Or has it hoarded God's blessings rather than extending them to all peoples? Either way, even though your people/your country might not seem as corrupt, as immoral, as evil as some other people group, judgment is still coming. God doesn't go lightly on those who claim to know Him and yet cause His reputation to be blasphemed. And when a country hoards God's outpouring of blessing, without passing it on, God simply shuts off the spigot.

The parallels in Scripture are obvious.

For the Sake of His Name

In the Old Testament God's people knew they were to "say among the nations, 'The Lord reigns'" (Psalm 96:10). In the most effective teaching method of the day—their memorized songs—they sang:

> Oh give thanks to the LORD, call upon His name;
> Make known His deeds among the peoples.
> Sing to the LORD, all the earth;
> Proclaim good tidings of His salvation from day to day.
> Tell of His glory among the nations,
> His wonderful deeds among all the peoples.
> Ascribe to the LORD, O families of the peoples,
> Ascribe to the LORD glory and strength.
> Ascribe to the LORD the glory due His name;
> Bring an offering, and come before Him;
> Worship the LORD in holy array.
> Let the heavens be glad, and let the earth rejoice;
> And let them say among the nations,
> "The LORD reigns" (1 Chronicles 16:8, 23–24, 28–29, 31).

But about 250 years after David wrote this song, Israel's ups and downs finally resulted in judgment.

The Big Fish and the Prostitute's Husband: Judgment in the North

Jonah and Hosea were God's spokesmen to the ten northern tribes of Israel. Jonah's message wasn't simply a story of the importance of personal obedience. His experience was the story of Israel's refusal to bless all the peoples of the earth—especially her enemies! Nineveh was the nerve center of the Assyrian dynasty, Israel's worst enemy and probably one of the most ruthless and savage people groups of all time. Jonah—representing the whole of Israel—didn't like the idea that God would ask such irritating questions as "Should I not have compassion on Nineveh?" (Jonah 4:11).

Jonah evidenced Israel's attitude toward blessing disdained peoples when he pouted at God's salvation of the Assyrian city: Nineveh's repentance "greatly displeased Jonah and he became angry . . . and said, 'Please LORD, was not this what I said while I was still in my own country? Therefore in order to forestall this [the salvation of Nineveh] I fled to Tarshish, for I knew that You are a gracious and compassionate God, slow to anger and abundant in lovingkindness, and one who relents concerning calamity'" (Jonah 4:1–2). Jonah and his people, the nation of Israel, knew that all nations would respond to the message they had of God's character. But they refused to proclaim Him. They would have to learn the hard way that you don't fool with the purpose of the God of the universe.

Hosea's experience of loving a faithless wife was a painful one-man-play that acted out the ten northern tribes' impending judgment. Hosea's message to the nation warned that unfaithfulness to God not only goes against the grain of His purpose, it also breaks His heart. Israel refused to be God's priests for the nations—sometimes obstinately, sometimes ignorantly: "My people are destroyed for lack of knowledge. Because you have rejected knowledge, I also will reject you from being My priest" (Hosea 4:6).

As Israel lost its sense of purpose as a kingdom of priests, it lost its distinction as a holy, set apart people: "Israel is swallowed up; they are now among the nations like a vessel in which no one delights" (Hosea 8:8). God showered them with blessings that they were to enjoy and to pass on in His name to all peoples. But they squandered all His blessings on the pursuit of their own gods: "Israel is a luxuriant vine; he produces fruit for himself. The more his fruit, the more altars he made; the richer his land, the better he made the sacred pillars" (Hosea 10:1).

God's call to Israel through Hosea was a warning of compassion. God would accomplish His purpose regardless of Israel's compliance. But why do it the hard way, knowing it would bring pain to God's people and pain to the very heart of God? "My heart is turned over within Me," God said. "All My compassions are kindled" (Hosea 11:8). And He insisted there was still time to repent and return to voluntarily represent His name: "The Lord, the God of hosts, the LORD is His name. Therefore, return to your God, observe kindness and justice, and wait for your God continually" (Hosea 12:5–6). Israel needed desperately to "return" in repentance, clean up her sins, and once again become the holy nation that could proclaim God's character of kindness and justice.

But out of stubbornness, or ignorance, she would not return.

More Trouble Down South

God's judgment against the southern kingdom of Judah was also predicted. Amos explained his dismal warnings with "Surely the Lord GOD does nothing unless He reveals His secret counsel to His servants the prophets" (Amos 3:7). These irritating prophets kept spoiling the people's good time with negative comments such as "Woe to those who are at ease in Zion and to those who feel secure . . . who recline on beds of ivory and sprawl on their couches and eat lambs from the flock. Who drink wine from sacrificial bowls" (Amos 6:1, 4, 6). God has a larger purpose than the comfort of His people.

Micah, whose name means "Who is like *YHWH*?" warned that when you are called by God's name, you don't challenge *Elohim-YHWH*: "Hear, O peoples, all of you; Listen, O earth and all it contains . . . the Lord is coming forth from His place. . . . The mountains will melt under Him. . . . All this is for the rebellion of Jacob" (Micah 1:2–5). About 150 years later Judah began to fulfill God's unchangeable purpose—the hard way.

Accomplishing God's purpose the hard way was not going to be easy for them. God promised to His people that in order to show His character as a God of holiness as well as compassion, "One third of you will die by plague or be consumed by famine among you, one third will fall by the sword around you, and one third I will scatter to every wind. . . . Moreover, I will make you a desolation and a reproach among the nations. . . . So it will be . . . a warning . . . to the nations who surround you" (Ezekiel 5:12, 14–15). With 95% of the world's trading routes passing through Israel, the nations of the earth would soon learn that you don't double-cross the God of Israel.

The prophet Ezekiel clearly spelled out God's rationale:

> Thus says the Lord GOD, "It is not for your sake, O house of Israel, that I am about to act, but for My holy name which you have profaned among the nations where you went. I will vindicate the holiness of My great name . . . which you have profaned in their midst. Then the nations will know that I am the LORD," declares the Lord GOD, "when I prove Myself holy among you in their sight" (Ezekiel 36:22–23; see also Ezekiel 39:21–23).

After the pain of the captivity, God himself explained that since His people "'refused to pay attention and turned a stubborn shoulder and stopped their ears from hearing'" and "'they made their hearts like flint . . . I scattered them with a storm wind among all the nations whom they have not known' " (Zechariah 7:11–12, 14).

God's Ongoing Twofold Program

Even when Israel refused to be a blessing to the nations, God carried on His predestined program. He used even these painful events of judgment to announce: "'Turn to Me and be saved, all the ends of the earth; for I am God, and there is no other. I have sworn by Myself, the word has gone forth from My mouth . . . and will not turn back. . . . "My purpose will be established, and I will accomplish all My good pleasure." . . . Truly I have spoken; truly I will bring it to pass. I have planned it, surely I will do it'" (Isaiah 45:22–23; 46:10–11).

Even as God's people underwent judgment the purposeful God of compassion promised that their role as His chosen people, as a light to the world's peoples ("the Gentiles"—all the nations other than Israel) would continue (see Isaiah 60:1–3) and be focused in the coming Servant (Isaiah 49:6).

God said,

> "Pay attention to Me, O My people; and give ear to Me, O My nation; for a law will go forth from Me, and I will set My justice for a light of the peoples. . . . The coastlands will wait for Me. . . . When the LORD restores Zion . . . the LORD has bared His holy arm in the sight of all the nations, that all the ends of the earth may see the salvation of our God" (Isaiah 51:4–5; 52:8–10).

God's unchangeable purpose would continue through His people, voluntarily or otherwise!

Even God's judgment on His people displayed God's character—His holiness and disdain of sin. He allowed them to be taken captive to Babylon and eventually used even their disobedience to further His unchangeable purpose to bless all nations.

Even in the context of judgment some individuals intently

served God's purpose in their generation. In captivity in Babylon, Daniel's witness to the character of God resulted in emperor Nebuchadnezzar's testimony to God's greatness (Daniel 4) and Darius's incredible proclamation "to all the peoples, nations and men of every language who were living in all the land. . . . I make a decree that in all the dominion of my kingdom men are to fear and tremble before the God of Daniel; for He is the living God and enduring forever . . . He delivers and rescues. . . ." (Daniel 6:25–27).

At the close of the 70 years of captivity God blessed His people again. The Persian ruler Cyrus acknowledged "the LORD, the God of heaven" and allowed about 50,000 Jews to return to their land laden with "silver and gold, with goods and cattle, together with a freewill offering for the house of God which is in Jerusalem" (Ezra 1:2, 4).

What did God's people do with these blessings? Almost 15 years after they arrived back in the land they still had done nothing about rebuilding God's house of prayer for the nations. They had used some of the proceeds of Cyrus's generosity to buy cedar wood from Lebanon. But instead of using it to build up God's house, they installed the new cedar paneling in their own homes! God sent the prophet Haggai to slap them awake: Did His people really want another round of judgment?

Scripture often suggests the imagery that God's temple is made up of living stones from every people—as some Jews and Gentiles alike join His family (see 2 Corinthians 6:16; Ephesians 2:11–22; 1 Peter 2:5). Many believers today patronizingly insist that it is not the time for God to finish building this temple made of some from every nation; we have to improve our own lives first. Some believers sequester most of God's blessings to pad their own nests, which makes a simple reading of Haggai's message a bit unnerving:

> A Message from GOD-of-the-Angel-Armies:
> "The people procrastinate. They say this isn't the right time to rebuild my Temple, the Temple of GOD."
> Shortly after that, GOD said more and Haggai spoke it:
> "How is it that it's the 'right time' for you to live in your fine new homes while the Home, GOD's Temple, is in ruins?"

And then a little later, GOD-of-the-Angel-Armies spoke out
again:

"Take a good, hard look at your life.
Think it over.
You have spent a lot of money,
but you haven't much to show for it.
You keep filling your plates,
but you never get filled up.
You keep drinking and drinking and drinking,
but you're always thirsty.
You put on layer after layer of clothes,
but you can't get warm.
And the people who work for you,
what are they getting out of it?
Not much—
a leaky, rusted-out bucket, that's what. . . .
Here's what I want you to do:
Climb into the hills and cut some timber.
Bring it down and rebuild the Temple.
Do it just for me. Honor me.
You've had great ambitions for yourselves,
but nothing has come of it.
The little you have brought to my Temple
I've blown away—there was nothing to it.
And why? . . . Because while you've run around,
caught up with taking care of your own houses,
my Home is in ruins"
(Haggai 1:2–6, 8–9 THE MESSAGE).

The New International Version translates the end of verse 6 in
a metaphor that feels eerily close to home: "You earn wages, only
to put them in a purse with holes in it."

Happily, God's people listened to Haggai's message, "obeyed
the voice of the LORD their God . . ." and "showed reverence for
the LORD." God reminded them, " 'I am with you,' " and
"stirred up . . . the spirit of all the remnant of the people; and
they came and worked on the house of the LORD of hosts, their
God" (Haggai 1:12–14).

As they worked to finally finish the temple four years later,
they doubtless remembered Solomon's proverb: "Surely there is
a future, and your hope will not be cut off" (Proverbs 23:18).

Their repentance didn't simply include a renouncing of sins; it also incorporated a return to God's clear purpose to finish building His temple. And so they resumed their journey on the path of blessing. Even though they had committed sins of commission and omission, they could repent and again sense hope for the future of their nation—hope like an anchor in the soul.

Of course, if God's people repent merely to receive more of God's blessing for themselves, to have easier lives, or simply to avoid judgment, nothing happens. The land isn't healed. But God's people can repent to receive more of God's "top-line" blessing in order to pass on "bottom-line" blessings to every people. They can turn from paneling their own houses with the resources God has provided. They can return to the task of building His temple of "living stones . . . built up as a spiritual house for a holy priesthood" (1 Peter 2:5). At that step of full repentance God's response is immediate: "'Take courage . . . and work; for I am with you. . . . My Spirit is abiding in your midst; do not fear!'" (Haggai 2:4–5).

Wouldn't it be wonderful if the people of God in your nation repented like that?

Devout Men From Every Nation

Later God orchestrated events in the lives of Ezra and Nehemiah to go back and rebuild the walls of Jerusalem. Why? God predicted through Jeremiah: "'Behold, I will bring to it [Jerusalem] health and healing, and I will heal them; and I will reveal to them an abundance of peace and truth.'" And why would God again bless His people in the rebuilt Jerusalem? "'It will be to Me a name of joy, praise and glory before all the nations of the earth which will hear of all the good that I do for them'" (Jeremiah 33:6, 9).

God accomplishes His purpose, and whether His people are willing to align themselves with that purpose or not, "He does according to His will in the host of heaven"—as He retakes Satan's counter-kingdom in the spiritual realm—"and among the inhabitants of earth"—as He brings men to himself through salvation (Daniel 4:35).

Even among those of God's people who stayed in Babylon

rather than return to Jerusalem, God pushed His agenda during the dispersion. The sweeping-saga scenes of the book of Esther have but one point: God broadcasts His powerful, redeeming character through the "satraps, the governors, and the princes of the provinces that extended from India [which some scholars say referred to *every* nation east of Babylon!] to Ethiopia [which figuratively meant Africa as a whole], 127 provinces, to every province according to its script, and to every people according to their language" (Esther 8:9).

God made sure that even these Jewish exiles clearly proclaimed "words of peace and truth" (Esther 9:30)—topics of God's blessing and character—so that all peoples could respond: "In each and every province and in each and every city . . . many among the peoples of the land became Jews" and "allied themselves with them" (Esther 8:17; 9:27).

In the ensuing 400 years until the birth of the Light, "Your salvation, which You have prepared in the presence of all peoples" (Luke 2:30–31), the number of God's people grew among the nations. Jewish missions to win proselytes (converts from other peoples who completely followed all Jewish rites) and "God-fearers" (converts who believed but were not circumcised) prospered until there were at the time of the early apostles "devout men from every nation under heaven" (Acts 2:5)!

God propels His purpose to offer salvation to every people, tribe, tongue, and nation—whether His people want to be blessed in the process or not!

To Whom Much Is Given

God has overwhelmingly blessed His people worldwide. Compare the mid–2004 resources of the global body of Christ with the projected 2025 numbers (in 2004 value of U.S. dollars):

	2004	2025
Unaffiliated Christians	106,665,000	113,890,000
Christians affiliated with a church	1,984,098,000	2,528,834,000

	2004	2025
*Great Commission Christians	682,026,000	876,525,000
Denominations	37,000	63,000
Congregations	3,663,000	5,035,000
Foreign-mission agencies	4,270	6,000
Christian workers	5,305,000	6,500,000
Foreign missionaries	439,000	550,000
Church members' income	US$16,590 billion	US$26,000 billion
Churches' income	US$130 billion	US$300 billion
Foreign mission agencies' income	US$20 billion	US$60 billion
Christian radio/TV stations	4,200	5,400
Computers in Christian use	430 million	1.7 billion

What do you think? Has God given His people the blessings and the resources to actively be a blessing to all the remaining unreached people groups of the earth?

Other blessings aren't quite so obvious since they're not necessarily quantified statistics. For example, the fact that we can travel to any point in the world within twenty-four hours is a phenomenon given to mankind in just the past couple of decades. More than 250 million Christians travel as tourists outside their own countries each year. Or consider the incredible blessings of being able to find out rare information about God's world via the World Wide Web, or to communicate easily across the world on the Internet and on mobile satellite telephones. The new computerized capability for the world's 300 Christian research institutes to communicate and compile data about God's harvest field is itself a blessed resource. World Christians are communicating as never before in more than 5,000 global Great Commission networks.

Often we need to rethink, to be creative in counting the blessings God has provided as resources for His global purpose—blessings such as getting old! The "graying" of Europe and North America, for example, is a tremendous resource for implementing God's plan to bless every people with the offer of salvation. As rest homes and nursing facilities expand with

*"Great Commission Christians" denotes committed believers who share their faith.
Source: *International Bulletin of Missionary Research,* January 2004.

record numbers of the elderly, some see longer life-spans as a curse of boredom and uselessness. But a worldview that focuses on God's unchangeable purpose sees the growing population of elderly believers as a significant resource expressly allowed by God for such a time as this.

The elderly can still work at reaching the world. At the time of Christ the average life-span was twenty-eight years. This wasn't much time to grow up, get educated, have a family, and figure out how to focus in a practical way on God's plan for the nations. Today's life-span in many countries in the world is nearly three times that figure. Today's believer has three times the number of years of growth and maturity to fight the good fight in the process of proclaiming the excellencies of His name.

The elderly can take time to pray around the world. No other population segment of Christians has more discretionary time for serious global prayer than experienced, mature, elderly believers!

God has blessed His people.

What are we doing with His resources? Running to panel our own houses while God's plan is to build His temple of living stones? We've been given much; and it's sometimes uncomfortable to think about how much is required to put us back on the pathway of blessing:

> How blessed all those in whom you live,
> whose lives become roads you travel;
> They wind through lonesome valleys, come upon brooks,
> discover cool springs and pools brimming with rain!
> God-traveled, these roads curve up the mountain, and
> at the last turn—Zion! God in full view!
> (Psalm 84:5–7 THE MESSAGE)

For Further Thought

1. Write out in your own words David's song from 1 Chronicles 16:18, 23–24, 28–29, 31.
2. Reread Haggai 1. Review the lists of blessings God has bestowed on His people. Then, as often as you can, pray for God's people to recognize the purpose of God's blessings.
3. Pray for breakthroughs among the Tuareg!

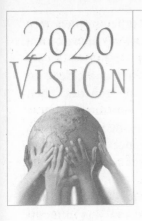

CHAPTER 9

A MESSIAH FOR ALL NATIONS:

Sprinting Through the New Testament

AFRICA

Tanzania➤

Tanzania. Canadian Clarence Duncan has bounced you over miles of dusty grassland driving east from the coast in Tanzania. The top of the Land Rover is open, and fine silt puffs each time you shift in your seat. It's a bright, hot day, and the breeze is so welcome you close your eyes and rest your head back as Clarence fights the wheel and the Rover bounces comfortably over the dirt road.

This is an unusual man. God has put him in an unusual place: in the middle of a solidly Islamic country in the middle of a solidly Islamic people group—the Yao. The Yao live in

Tanzania, Mozambique, Malawi, and a few other southeastern African countries. Clarence has told you how he arrived in a village when he first came back in 1985.

He had called a meeting with the village chief and elders, sat before them, and gone through the customary pleasantries. Then the chief asked, "What is your name?" We've learned the importance of names in the non-Western cultures of the world, right?

Clarence had simply answered, "Mr. Clarence."

The council looked at each other. The chief asked, "Why are you here?"

Again, very simply, Clarence had answered, "I want to tell your people about *Isa Al Mahsi*." And permission was immediately granted.

Now Clarence is explaining over the roar of the Rover: "Then a couple of months later when the chief realized he could trust me, he said, 'Do you know why we allowed you to stay?' And I said, 'Never thought about it.' He said, 'Twenty-one years ago a very old Yao man came to our village and called for a meeting as you did. When we asked him his name this Yao man said, "Mr. Clarence"—which isn't an African name at all! When we asked him why he came, he said, "I want to tell your people about *Isa Al Mahsi*." These were your very words. Twenty-one years ago Mr. Clarence led four of our villagers to follow Jesus. So we ran them out of the village. And we killed Mr. Clarence. The reason we allowed you to stay was we were afraid.'"

Then Clarence's British lilt rolls right into another story that took place just two years ago. Some of the Yao people were coming to Christ, and a church had been planted. The Islamic authorities in the region tried to deport him and his family, but God intervened. Then he hits you with another one of those goose-bump revelations of the way God is orchestrating events all over the globe to bless every people group with redemption in Christ.

Clarence says:

> One January morning, I think it was the fourteenth, about ten in the morning, up our driveway comes a whole retinue of twenty-four Muslim leaders from around the country. The whole country! Behind them many of the people from our village followed to watch what was obvi-

ously going to be some sort of public spectacle. I didn't want that, so I asked the Muslim leaders to send the people away and I would do so with the Christians. After some discussion they agreed.

After the greetings and our meal together we all sat down in a large rectangular room adjacent to our house. I was against one wall, with twenty-three of the Muslim leaders along the other walls. The head of the leaders sat in the middle of the room opposite me.

He said they had come to ask me a few questions about the Christian faith.

"That's fine," I said, "but so that you will know that the answers to your questions are not things I invent, I will read the answers from the Bible." I gave them each a Bible in the trade language and told them where they could read along with me before I read a passage.

The head sheik sitting opposite me began the questioning. The others sat silently observing.

The first question was "Why do you Christians say that there are three gods?" The answer was a simple one. I told them the page number for Deuteronomy 6:4–5: "Hear, O Israel! The LORD is our God, the LORD is one! You shall love the LORD your God with all your heart and with all your soul and with all your might." And I mentioned to them that these are the words *Isa* (Jesus) quoted when He spoke to the scribes in Mark 12:29, regarding the "greatest commandment." Jesus himself told us there is one God.

The barrage of questions went on until about lunchtime, when the meeting was suddenly adjourned. They went outside for their Friday noon prayers and then came back in for more questions.

As the afternoon wore on the leader kept asking more questions. There was one question about the Trinity that was hard for me to answer using Scripture alone. I wanted to explain it in a graphic, visual way. But in order to do that I had to stand up, walk around, and gesture.

About five o'clock in the afternoon they abruptly decided the meeting was over and left.

The one who had asked all the questions, Sheik Abu Bakr, hung back until we were alone in the room. He asked quietly, "Would you come see me next week?" I nodded, and he left.

When I saw him the next week he looked at me carefully and said, "Do you know why we came to visit you last week?"

A bit puzzled by the question, I answered, "Certainly. You came to ask me questions about the Christian faith."

"No," Abu said, "we came to kill you."

In the African culture you never tell someone that you intend to hurt him; you especially wouldn't let him know of your intention to kill him!

Abu continued, "Do you remember when a group tried to throw you out of the country—and it didn't work? The Christian church here grew so much we Muslim leaders knew we had to get you out one way or another. We decided that the only way was to kill you.

"We spent three days consulting our witchcraft as to how we would do this before we came to see you. Finally we decided on our plan: We would each sit in a specific place in the room, with our medicine in our pocket. We had even invited the people of the village to watch what would happen. When we asked you questions our magic would be so powerful you would be struck dumb and would not be able to answer the questions. Then you would be laughed at and humiliated. And after a while, you would fall to the ground paralyzed, and then die.

"But when we asked you the first question, you kept talking and talking and talking! We thought, 'Our medicine isn't working.' When we went out in the middle of the day, we consulted our magic again and came in and sat in different places to improve the power. But still it would not work.

"Do you remember when you explained to us the Trinity? You got up and walked around, waving your arms, and talking and talking! After that we decided you had a more powerful Spirit who was protecting you. So we decided there was no use trying to kill you and gave up and left."

Needless to say I was quite surprised to hear this story.

Abu broke into my thoughts, "I want to become a Christian."

Well, that shocked me more than anything! I said, "Why?" And the sheik told me this story.

"When I was a teenager, in our village we were not Muslim people and we were not Christian. We were

Achewa people with our own religion. Behind our village was a hill where I would often go to pray.

"One day I was on that hill praying. Suddenly all around me was a blinding light. Out of this light I saw a big hand coming toward me holding an open book. I looked at the book and saw writing on the page. A Voice told me to read. I protested that I could not read, never having been to school. The Voice again told me to read. So I did. And suddenly the book and the hand disappeared.

"I ran back to my village and all the people were looking for me, thinking I had died on that hill! They asked about a fire they had seen up there. When I told them the story they laughed at me saying, 'You can't read!'

"Someone got a book and I began to read! Then people came from all around to find out more about what happened and ask questions. The Muslim authorities found out about me and I was trained in the ways of Islam. Soon all of our village became Muslim. For fifteen years I was the greatest debater against the Christians."

He paused and I asked him, "Why are you telling me all of this?"

He said, "You remember when I asked you the first question about why Christians believe in three gods? Your answer was Deuteronomy chapter six, verse four."

"That's right," I said.

Sheik Abu Bakr looked me straight in the eye and said, "That was the same passage that this Voice on the mountain showed me. At that moment I knew that the God you were talking about was the True God!"

Talk about a shock! I asked, "Then why did you keep asking me all those questions the whole day?"

"Because," he smiled, "I wanted all these Muslim leaders to know what the Christians believe and I wanted them to hear it from your holy Scriptures. The whole day I pretended unbelief so that I could ask more questions. Now I want to become a Christian."

You're not even near the Duncans' village yet, but you've already been blessed by what God is doing among the Yao. And you're also jealous; wouldn't it be wonderful to be used by God so specifically in His great plan to bless a people group, as was Clarence Duncan?! Then you realize you're getting the idea.

God's historic Great Commission given to Abraham 4,000 years ago does include you, your life, and your place in history. God can use every believer just as wonderfully as He has the Duncans! But how?

The apostle Paul says, "To each one of us grace [*giftedness* is an accurate synonym] was given according to the measure of Christ's gift. And He gave some as apostles, and some as prophets, and some as evangelists, and some as pastors and teachers, for the equipping of the saints for the work of service." For what purpose? "to the building up of the body of Christ" (Ephesians 4:7, 11–12).

We each have a function, a place (see Romans 12:3–8; 1 Corinthians 12). Paul writes, "All are not apostles, are they?" (1 Corinthians 12:29). Apostle means "sent one"; and you simply weren't sent to the Yao. At least not at this point. Your mandate is to fulfill your role in the body now so it can function, "being fitted and held together . . . according to the proper working of each individual part" (Ephesians 4:16).

And what is the body of Christ doing? It's going about the Father's business! Just as Jesus was in His life on earth.

What does the New Testament say about this ongoing story of the Bible? Is Jesus the Messiah for all peoples?

Our meager glimpse at the Old Testament's solid predictions of Christ as the Servant who "will sprinkle many nations" (Isaiah 52:15) has at least prepared us to take a fresh glance at the familiarity of the New Testament. Is God's unchangeable purpose an obvious theme running through the next 26 sections of the story of the Bible? Let's sprint through the New Testament.

The Gospels

Jesus was born as a light to the Gentiles

John the Baptist was celebrated at birth as the forerunner of the Christ who was coming to "SHINE UPON THOSE WHO SIT IN DARKNESS AND THE SHADOW OF DEATH" (Luke 1:79). Anyone listening to this song of Zacharias knew that the passage in Isaiah referred to God making Galilee of the Gentiles glorious by the coming of the Messiah (see Isaiah 9). Remember, the term *Gentile* means every people group other than the Jews.

Likewise, Simeon's announcement of Jesus' birth clearly confirmed the all-nations scope of the Messiah: "For my eyes have seen Your salvation, which You have prepared in the presence of all peoples, A LIGHT OF REVELATION TO THE GENTILES, and the glory of Your people Israel" (Luke 2:30–32). Simeon also quoted from Isaiah: "I will also make You a light of the nations so that My salvation may reach to the end of the earth" (Isaiah 49:6).

This same passage was repeated later as Paul and Barnabas arrived in the town of Pisidian Antioch to spread the blessing (Acts 13:46–47).

After the reading of the Law and the Prophets in the synagogue, Paul proclaimed the all-nations message of God to the "sons of Abraham's family and those among them who fear God." Paul presented the fact that the Christ had died and rose again to provide salvation for "everyone who believes"—not just the Jews. He warned his Jewish listeners not to scoff at the blessing being offered to everyone; then he quoted Habakkuk 1:5, "Look among the nations! Observe! Be astonished! Wonder! Because *I am* doing something in your days—you would not believe if you were told." (See Acts 13:41.)

When the following Sabbath brought retaliation from jealous Jews, Paul and Barnabas replied that they were following God's explicit command. They simply quoted the verse Simeon shouted at Jesus' birth: "'I HAVE PLACED YOU AS A LIGHT FOR THE GENTILES, THAT YOU MAY BRING SALVATION TO THE END OF THE EARTH'" (Acts 13:47). The result? The word of the Lord was being spread throughout the whole region!

Jesus' early ministry was to the Jew first but also to all peoples

Jesus could have made the center of Judaism in Jerusalem His headquarters. Instead, He initially based His ministry in Galilee of the Gentiles. His first miracle was in Cana. In His first sermon in Nazareth (Luke 4:24–30) He reminded His Jewish and Gentile audience that the great faith He called men to was best exemplified in those from other people groups:

Elijah was sent to a widow woman of the Sidon people (1 Kings 17).

Naaman, a Syrian military officer whose people were merci-lessly destroying Israel at that very time, was healed of leprosy because of the intercession of a little Israeli servant-girl (2 Kings 5:1–14).

In His hometown area of "Galilee of the gentiles," Jesus, "seeing the people . . . felt compassion for them. . . . Then He said to His disciples, 'The harvest is plentiful, but the workers are few. Therefore beseech the Lord of the harvest to send out workers into His harvest'" (Matthew 9:36–38; see the parallel passage in Luke 10:2). His heart not only yearns for His people; God feels compassion for the multitudes of every people group on earth.

An incisive translation of the phrase *send out* is "thrust out" or even "cast out"! It is the same verb used when Jesus drove out the temple money changers and cast out demons. Sometimes God's action in getting laborers active in His harvest will be a bit disconcerting—even painful—to the "thrust-out" workers!

Jesus promised two problems in the worldwide harvest: The harvest will be vast, and the workers will be few. His answer? Pray!

When Jesus sent out the twelve He strategically commanded them to go to the "lost sheep of Israel" (see Matthew 10). Warn-ing the nation of impending judgment, the disciples were not to spend time in what they later would do—preaching to other peoples. Even in that context of Israel's doom, however, the dis-ciples were to be aware that every other people would be watch-ing how God handled His reputation among His people: "'You will even be brought before governors and kings for My sake, as a testimony to them and to the Gentiles'" (Matthew 10:18).

Later Jesus sent out the seventy disciples (Luke 10:1–20) to every city He would visit—whether Jewish or not. First, twelve, possibly representing the twelve tribes of Israel, were sent exclu-sively to the Jews to warn that nation of judgment. Then sev-enty, possibly representing the seventy nations formed at the Tower of Babel, were sent out to call all people groups to repent-ance.

Jesus' later ministry included all peoples

Jesus later spent His time in Jewish areas. So it is noteworthy that so many of His contacts were with individuals of other peoples:

He healed the Gadarene demoniac (Matthew 8:28–34).

He noted that a Samaritan was the only one of ten lepers who returned to thank Him for healing him (Luke 17:12–19).

He explained to a Samaritan woman that God was to be worshiped in spirit and in truth (John 4:5–42).

A Canaanite woman's daughter was released from demon-possession because of the mother's great faith (Matthew 15:22–28). Reading this remarkable passage carefully, we see that Jesus' initial silence and statement of exclusivity ("I was sent only to . . . Israel") was totally out of character for the One born the Light of the Gentiles. We can almost sense His, and the woman's, facetiousness as Jesus taught His prejudiced disciples (see verse 23) a critical lesson: God is interested in freeing all peoples from the powers of Satan's counter-kingdom.

The Roman centurion's servant was healed as Jesus marveled at his faith (Matthew 8:5–13). Jesus reminded His audience that "many will come from east and west, and recline at the table with Abraham, Isaac and Jacob in the kingdom of heaven" (Matthew 8:11).

A group of Greek God-fearers pleaded with Philip, "Sir, we wish to see Jesus." And it was to this group Jesus first announced clearly His coming death: "And I, if I am lifted up from the earth, will draw all men to Myself" (John 12:21, 32). All men.

In the final events of His life on earth, Jesus acted on behalf of every people

Events from the last week before Jesus' crucifixion to His ascension teem with references to the all-nations theme of the story of the Bible:

Christ entered Jerusalem, "humble, and mounted on a donkey. . . . And He will speak peace to the nations" (Zechariah 9:9–10).

Jesus cleansed the temple's Court of the Gentiles, throwing out the hawkers and money changers, and saying, "Is it not written, 'MY HOUSE SHALL BE CALLED A HOUSE OF PRAYER FOR ALL THE NATIONS'?" (Mark 11:17).

The final week before the cross is when He answered clearly the question "What will be the sign of Your coming, and of the end of the age?" (Matthew 24:3). His answer? Jesus tells of several "birth pangs" and then says, "This gospel of the kingdom shall be preached in the whole world for a witness to all the nations, and then the end will come" (Matthew 24:14).

As Mary anointed Jesus at the house in Bethany Jesus promised that every people would hear of her devotion "wherever this gospel is preached in the whole world" (Matthew 26:13).

Let us never forget the global significance of Jesus' death for the sins of the whole world (1 John 2:2). And in the gospel of John: "For God so loved the world, that He gave His only begotten Son, that whoever believes in Him shall not perish, but have eternal life" (John 3:16).

After His resurrection Jesus patiently explained the whole of Scripture to the two disciples on the road to Emmaus and later to all His disciples (Luke 24:13–49). His nutshell commentary included all nations:

> He opened their minds to understand the Scriptures, and He said to them, "Thus it is written, that the Christ should suffer and rise again from the dead the third day, and that repentance for forgiveness of sins would be proclaimed in His name to all the nations, beginning from Jerusalem" (Luke 24:45–47).

How clear can the story of the Bible be? Forgiveness of sins should be proclaimed in His name to all the nations!

As Jesus met for the final time with His disciples in Galilee of the Gentiles, He gave what we call the Great Commission:

> "Go therefore and make disciples of all the nations, baptizing them in the name of the Father and the Son and the Holy Spirit, teaching them to observe all that I commanded you; and lo, I am with you always, even to the end of the age" (Matthew 28:19–20).

By now we know that this command was nothing new. It was not simply an afterthought of what the disciples could do with their spare time until He returned. This command was a clear, forceful repetition of the message God had been giving since His imperative 2,000 years before when He had told Jacob, "'In you and in your descendants shall all the families of the earth be blessed. Behold, I am with you'" (Genesis 28:14–15a).

Acknowledging this familiar passage as the Great re-Commission, let's think carefully through what Jesus actually said:

"All authority has been given to Me in heaven and on earth" (Matthew 28:18). Jesus has disarmed all rulers and authorities in the heavenly realm of Satan's battling counter-kingdom (Colossians 2:15 and Hebrews 2:14–15). The peoples of the earth no longer have to be prisoners of Satan's darkness. They remain enslaved only because of ignorance of Christ's freedom or because of obstinance in deference to Satan.

Because of the "therefore" (Matthew 28:19), we are commanded to make disciples. The "go" in this passage is not actually an imperative in the Greek text; it is more accurately an assumption: "As you are going . . ." The force of the entire text is the command "make disciples"—followers, learners.

What is the object of the command? "Every *ethne*"—all the peoples, nations, Gentiles, families of the earth. What complicated the 1611 King James Version of the Great re-Commission, of course, was its parallel passage in Mark 16:15: "Go ye into all the world and preach the gospel to every creature." No wonder many Christians think Christ's command is only idealistic; telling the Gospel to *every individual* on earth is a hopeless task! The Mark passage is perhaps better translated "to all creation"— a much more general term than our idea of every individual creature.

This is strategically important because Jesus was not reiterating the Commission as an ideal; He was dead serious. The Great Commission is about taking the news of the blessing to each *ethne*. Those who respond are to be baptized into the name of the Father, Son, and Holy Spirit, and they're to be taught to observe all that Christ commanded—including this command!

As outsiders, we are to bring the Gospel to every nation; then it is those new disciples' responsibility to be witnesses in their own society. They know their own language, their own culture; they have their own natural networks. And as they respond to God's ancient offer of redemption in Christ, they come to know the meaning of "Blessed is the nation whose God is the LORD" (Psalm 33:12).

The Acts of the Apostles

As usual, the disciples were stuck on top-line blessing as they asked the ascending Christ, "'Lord, is it at this time You are restoring the kingdom to Israel?'" (Acts 1:6). In other words, "Are we now going to get the whole bundle of blessings promised us as God's chosen people?"

Jesus, of course, replies with a clear-cut statement that balances top-line blessing: "It is not for you to know times or epochs which the Father has fixed by His own authority; but you will receive power when the Holy Spirit has come upon you—" and bottom-line responsibility: "and you shall be My witnesses both in Jerusalem, and in all Judea and Samaria, and even to the remotest part of the earth'" (Acts 1:7–8).

The remainder of the Acts of the Apostles can be seen in light of this: God's blessing on His people to bless all peoples.

The Day of Pentecost modeled the plan

You're in Jerusalem. You're one of the God-fearers who by faith is trusting in the God of the Jews. You're fresh off the ship from Cnidus in Phrygia—in what would later become western Turkey.

Seasickness was nothing compared to the disorientation you feel amid the rush of dusty travelers and locals weaving in and out among each other in the crowd-packed walkways of the market. Children shriek in a language foreign to you, some bright-robed market hawkers shout, "Melons! Fresh melons!" in Greek, the language you've learned to worship in back home at the synagogue.

But the conversations, the remarks, and the shouts all around you as you wade through the striped-robed crowd are in languages you've never heard before. You constantly remind yourself that no matter how foreign you feel in this place, they're not really all talking about you.

Suddenly a wild windstorm blows in off the desert, but protected here in the market alleyways, you don't even feel a puff of wind.

Then you hear it wafting above the tumult: Up at the next corner a man is standing on the back of a cart speaking in pure, unaccented Phrygian.

You rush forward to get a closer look. Could it be that other God-fearers from your homeland are here too? Now you see that most of the marketplace crowd is surging toward the same corner, everyone speaking in a different language. It is an effort to see above the milling turbans of dozens of men. Women are also gathering around, and finally you are close enough to notice the swarthy features of the man—he is a Jew! He's explaining that the promise of God's long-awaited blessing has now come to you!

"'Repent, and each of you be baptized in the name of Jesus Christ for the forgiveness of your sins; and you will receive the gift of the Holy Spirit. For the promise is for you and your children and for all who are far off'" (Acts 2:38–39).

You know that you are one whom the Scriptures refer to as "far off." The promise of the Abrahamic blessing has come to you!

Then the bottom line hits you. If you and any other Phrygians here today are the first to hear of this fulfillment, who is responsible for carrying the news of this blessing back home?

So Pentecost demonstrated God's blessing on His people, the disciples on whom the power of the promised Spirit fell, and on every nation. The Day of Pentecost proclaimed the fact that God's blessing was to drench "devout men from every nation under heaven"—and apparently all the nations were represented in the one city of Jerusalem at that incredible point in history (Acts 2:5). God showed that the New Testament plan was the same as the Old: God blesses His people to be a blessing to every people.

The early sermons hinged on God's outpouring of blessing on the Jew first, and also on all peoples

In the days following Pentecost the headstrong fisherman Simon Peter eloquently articulated the order of God's blessing in a sermon to the Jewish crowd gathered at the portico of Solomon, a porch along the temple's Court of the Gentiles:

"All the prophets . . . announced these days. 'It is you who are the sons of the prophets and of the covenant which God made with your fathers, saying to Abraham, "AND IN YOUR SEED ALL THE FAMILIES OF THE EARTH SHALL BE

BLESSED." For you first, God raised up His Servant and sent Him to bless you by turning every one of you from your wicked ways'" (Acts 3:24–26).

God's people were blessed to be a blessing. The apostle Paul, speaking years later in a synagogue in Phrygia, confirms this order: "'It was necessary that the Word of God would be spoken to you first; since . . . "I HAVE PLACED YOU AS A LIGHT FOR THE GENTILES"'" (Acts 13:46–47).

As usual, God's people—even the venerated early disciples—hesitated to bless the nations

Jerusalem was the most strategic, central place to reach the people group called the Jews. So although it was not home to most of the early disciples, that is where they focused their early ministry of passing on the blessing.

Christ orders us to expend the power of the Spirit by being witnesses in strategic places within our own people group. Be careful if someone's interpretation of Jesus' command to "be witnesses" suggests that *Jerusalem* meant "hometown" to his disciples, that no shift, no movement, no change of lifestyle is necessary to become an obedient disciple. Jesus always prods us out of the status quo.

Also, Jesus had told the disciples to be witnesses to Him "both" in Jerusalem and beyond—not first in Jerusalem, and then when they had things well under control there, to the ends of the earth.

But as Jonah of old, the disciples would not budge. And God initiated His age-old motivation system to bless all nations whether His people cooperated voluntarily or not. "A great persecution began against the church in Jerusalem." And the predictable result? "They were all scattered throughout the regions of Judea and Samaria." The Lord sent them exactly where He said He would—into all Judea and Samaria. Why? To accomplish His unchangeable purpose: "Therefore, those who had been scattered went about preaching the word" (Acts 8:1, 4).

The infamous Cultural Revolution in the People's Republic of China in the 1960s and 1970s parallels this persecution account in the book of Acts. Beginning in the 1960s the Chinese Communist Party "purged" their culture of millions of intellectuals and Western-influenced citizens. Tens of thousands of these persecuted people were Christians. As they were forcibly relocated or as they fled from China's cities to remote, rural areas, they carried the Gospel with them.

Before the time of the Cultural Revolution it was estimated that there were about 2,000 unreached people groups within the political borders of China. But after 1976, when China opened somewhat to the West, researchers were astounded to find that possibly one half of these unreached people groups had been reached with the Gospel during these terrible years of persecution. God had spread His Word from people group to people group through persecution.

Notice that Philip was one of those scattered. He's probably the classic example of God drafting someone into His great cause. If you're a deacon in a local church, take special note. Watch and tremble at Philip's progress in aligning with God's purpose to bless the nations: First, Philip is chosen to be a local church deacon (Acts 6:5).

Then we see him becoming (pushed into being) a cross-cultural evangelist (Acts 8:5). Samaritans were considered to be half-Jewish and half-Assyrian, so Philip's preaching had to cross some cultural barriers of custom and acceptance. But as he preached in his own language to this culturally near people, his ministry would be considered at this point to be evangelism—sharing the Gospel within your own or a culturally similar people group.

A few verses later Philip is thrust out into the Gaza Desert to proclaim Christ as the suffering Servant of Isaiah to the Ethiopian eunuch (Acts 8:26–39). And as he explained the Word beginning at Isaiah 53, he undoubtedly kept on reading and explaining until the Nubian was spellbound to hear:

> Let not the foreigner who has joined himself to the LORD say, "The Lord will surely separate me from His people." Neither let the eunuch say, "Behold, I am a dry tree." For thus says the LORD, "To the eunuchs who keep My sabbaths, and choose what pleases Me . . . to them I will give in My house and within My walls a memorial, and a name better than that of sons and daughters; I will give them an everlasting name which will not be cut off. . . .

Their burnt offerings and their sacrifices will be acceptable on My altar; for My house will be called a house of prayer for all the peoples" (Isaiah 56:3, 5, 7).

Would it be any wonder if the eunuch suddenly whistled his chariot to a stop and exclaimed, "Why didn't they tell me this back at the synagogue? The way I heard it, I thought God loved the Jews more than any other people! I thought I had to renounce my whole cultural heritage and become a Jew to become acceptable to the God of Abraham, Isaac, and Jacob!" Actually, he said, "'Look! Water! What prevents me from being baptized?'" (Acts 8:36).

And so Philip was drawn by God through the training of serving as a deacon and an evangelist to eventually bless another people. As he reached across distinct cultural barriers to the Nubian, Philip fulfilled a mission. He was a missionary to another people group. And the Good News spread into Africa.

After the whole theme of Old Testament Scripture, after Jesus' ministry and final words to keep passing on the blessing, the apostles were still reluctant to believe God was longing to bless the Gentiles as well as the Jews.

Even after Peter's all-nations sermon just after Pentecost, he needed a distinct vision from God to offer the Good News to the Gentile family of Cornelius (Acts 10). Three times God reminded Peter in the vision that His unchangeable plan was to bless His people in order to bless every nation. As if thumped over the head with the message of the vision, Peter says, "I most certainly understand now that God is not one to show partiality, but in every *ethne* the man who fears Him and does what is right is welcome to Him" (Acts 10:34–35).

What was the other disciples' response to the Caesareans' (non-Jews) salvation in Christ? Was it rejoicing? Excitement that God's obvious plan since Genesis 12:3 was unfolding before their very eyes? No, they "took issue" with Peter. Peter shrugged, "Who was I that I could stand in God's way?" Then the noble, respected-throughout-history early disciples "when they heard this . . . quieted down and glorified God, saying, 'Well then, God has granted to the Gentiles also the repentance that leads to life'" (Acts 11:17–18). But they didn't give up their top-line grasp easily.

A whole council had to be called to iron out more of this unnerving business of God having His way in blessing other people groups! At the Council of Jerusalem, years after Pentecost, the Jewish-based church was still mostly concerned about itself (Acts 15).

Peter tried another run at convincing the Jerusalem leadership that God had indeed intended that the Great Commission be taken literally, that "'He made no distinction between us and them'" (Acts 15:9). Paul and Barnabas related what God was doing among the Gentiles; finally, James, the half-brother of Jesus, had to appeal to Scripture to break through their unbelief: "'God first concerned Himself about taking from among the Gentiles a people for His name. With this the words of the Prophets agree, "I WILL REBUILD THE TABERNACLE OF DAVID . . . SO THAT THE REST OF MANKIND MAY SEEK THE LORD, AND ALL THE GENTILES WHO ARE CALLED BY MY NAME"'" (Acts 15:13–17).

So it was that the early church leadership finally grasped the idea that God would accomplish His will to bless every people on earth. And who were they, that they could stand in God's way?

The Epistles

The epistles of the New Testament are familiar to most believers as rich ground for understanding doctrine and growing in Christ.

Christian growth has a distinct earthly purpose

Within the light of the theme of the story of the Bible we have to ask ourselves, "Why work at understanding doctrine and growing in Christ?"

Maybe we would automatically answer, "So our lives will be better" or "To become more like Christ." Both of these answers are true. Partially.

But if God simply wanted us to know doctrine "even as we are known," to no longer "see through a glass darkly" (1 Corinthians 13:12), to be "holy and blameless before Him" (Ephesians 1:4), wouldn't it make sense to swoop us away from the sludge of sin and the irritations of life in a fallen, Satan-plagued earth?

Or does God have a very distinct purpose for leaving us on earth? A custom-designed niche for us to fill in His unchangeable purpose?

And doesn't it make sense that since God uses humans in His plan, He wants us clean and equipped and obedient?

God admonishes us to be students of the Word, to rightly divide the Word of truth so that we will be transformed by it and use it to transform others! God orders husbands and wives to learn to live with each other according to knowledge and to love each other not just so they'll have rosy, glorious lives on beds of ease and prosperity; strong marriages are essential for a Christian couple to tackle the strongholds of Satan in order to work toward God's unchangeable purposes. God asks us to bear one another's burdens so we can get on with the task at hand. God instructs us to conduct ourselves with holiness and propriety not so we'll feel superior or lead charmed lives, but so that His name will be exalted among the world's *ethne*—our own included.

God wants us to know why He is gracious to us, why He blesses us and causes His face to shine upon us: It's *so that* His way may be known on the earth, His salvation among all peoples (Psalm 67:1–2).

The meat of the epistles is not intended for our blessing alone. For example, Paul wrote at the beginning of the deep, doctrinal book of Romans that he had received much from the Lord for the sake of others: "Paul, a servant of Jesus Christ . . . by whom we have received grace and apostleship for obedience to the faith among all nations for His name . . ." (Romans 1:1, 5 NKJV).

Near the end of his letter, Paul shares the vision of his life: "Thus I aspired to preach the gospel, not where Christ was already named . . . but as it is written, 'THEY WHO HAD NO NEWS OF HIM SHALL SEE, AND THEY WHO HAVE NOT HEARD SHALL UNDERSTAND'" (Romans 15:20–21).

And at the end of the book, Paul reemphasizes the reason why the teaching is critical. The Spirit wanted the Roman believers to be clear about "the revelation of the mystery which has been kept secret . . . but now is . . . made known to all the nations, leading to obedience of faith" (Romans 16:25–26).

The epistles are written to bless us with wisdom and strength because God has a distinct job for each of us. And in some indirect or direct way, it has to do with the people groups of our era who have not been blessed with the offer of salvation in Jesus Christ.

Christian growth prepares us for our roles

The apostle Paul affirms the unity of believers in Christ in remarkable passages such as Ephesians 2 and 3. He reminds his readers from people groups other than the Jews that at one time they were "strangers to the covenants of promise, having no hope and without God in the world." He affirms their position as "fellow citizens with the saints," as those living stones "being built together into a dwelling of God in the Spirit" (Ephesians 2:12, 19, 22).

Paul then says that this melding of all believers into one body had been a mystery "which in other generations was not made known to the sons of men, as it has now been revealed" (Ephesians 3:5). Then he spells out that mystery:

> To be specific, that the Gentiles are fellow heirs and fellow members of the body, and fellow partakers of the promise . . . so that the manifold wisdom of God might now be made known through the church to the rulers and the authorities in the heavenly places. This was in accordance with the eternal purpose which He carried out in Christ Jesus our Lord. (Ephesians 3:6, 10–11)

The Jews had known for 2,000 years that God's plan was to bless every people group on earth. That they often ignored their bottom-line responsibility doesn't prove they were ignorant of it. In the same way, New Testament believers can often thoroughly ignore the mandate of the Great Commission while being fully aware of it. That God would bless all peoples was not the mystery.

To the Israelites of old, the mystery was that this blessing would bring these "heathen" *ethne* into unity with His chosen people! God's chosen Hebrew-Jewish people would not only pass on His blessing but would have as fellow family members those from every people, tribe, tongue, and nation who were saved by grace! This equal status was uncomfortable news; this was a head-scratching mystery.

Many other passages in the epistles of the New Testament give more insight into God's heart for the Gentiles/nations/peoples/*ethne* of the earth. Yet even further doctrinal insight hardly compares with the brilliant vision of the fulfillment of God's plan.

The End

There is an end to the story of the Bible. Jesus said simply, "This gospel of the kingdom shall be preached in the whole world for a witness to all the nations, and then the end will come" (Matthew 24:14).

Regardless of your eschatology or your understanding of prophecy, the end of the story of the Bible records the fact that the apostle John saw the finale of God's global plan:

> And they sang a new song: "You are worthy to take the scroll and to open its seals, because you were slain, and with your blood you purchased men for God from every tribe and language and people and nation. You have made them to be a kingdom and priests to serve our God, and they will reign on the earth" (Revelation 5:9–10 NIV).

> After this I looked and there before me was a great multitude that no one could count, from every nation, tribe, people and language, standing before the throne and in front of the Lamb. (Revelation 7:9 NIV)

The New Testament confirms the depth of God's heart for the whole world. It reveals the central point of history in which God as Man offers himself as the Sacrifice. And the New Testament clarifies the task: God is reaching mankind through people groups—one by one—and there will be an end to that process.

For nearly 2,000 years, since the close of New Testament events, God has been inexorably accomplishing His unchangeable purpose. In quiet but amazing ways God has been disabling Satan's false rulership and redeeming men and women in groups such as the Yao—who have been without God and without hope.

For Further Thought

1. List the New Testament references mentioned in this chapter. Then review each one as a slower follow-up study through the New Testament.

2. Share this chapter's opening story as a source of "strong encouragement, sure and steadfast"(Hebrews 6:18–19) with another believer who needs to be reminded that God is on the throne, and He is accomplishing His perfect purpose in every detail of all our lives.

CHAPTER 10

THE HISTORY OF THE WORLD—TAKE TWO:

God's Purpose Through the Ages

The Amazon. It's midday, but you can't see the sun above the canopy of foliage a hundred feet above you. You're almost panting as the Jeep under you bucks like a wild horse along the track. "It must be the—ah—heat or something. Can we stop for a break?" you ask. The muffler is broken, and your head rings with the roar and exhaust. You've heard about the phenomenal growth of Christianity in Latin America, and you can't wait to see for yourself.

The tall man in the driver's seat nods and pulls to a stop. He revs the engine and switches off the ignition to the palpable silence of the jungle. He steps off to the side of the four-foot-wide muck he's been calling the road. "It's your jet lag. Don't worry about it. The heat takes it out of you too. Let me check you for bugs."

It's probably about 100° F and 99% humidity in the dripping forest of the central Amazon Basin. You swing your backpack off your shoulders and wish there were a dry place to sit—other than that board seat in the back of the Jeep. You notice your host smiling as he lifts your arms and pulls your khaki collar away to check your neck. Your skin crawls at the prospect of insects burrowing into your body within a matter of minutes. Your smile probably looks more like a grimace. "Just a breather, all right?" you beg. "My kidneys feel like they've been worked over by Muhammad Ali."

Maybe with the ulterior motive of prolonging your rest break, you ask, "Now, I heard some of the story from your students, but what really happened in this village?"

"What did the students say?" He stretches. You thought missionaries no longer took on the "Indiana Jones" look, but this South African anthropologist-ecologist, Donald Richards, looks the part exactly. All he needs is a whip.

"Well, a couple of them said they were riding on a bus after your training session at the school, and a wealthy landowner's personal secretary overheard them talking about ecological principles in caring for the rain forest's environment. Then she set up a meeting with the landowner for you."

"Yes," he says. "We met, and we couldn't believe it when he donated 40,000 hectares—a hectare is about two and a half acres. He wants us to maintain the area as sort of a buffer zone to keep development damage to a minimum."

Donald Richards is warming to the story, you think, as you mop your forehead.

He continues, "So in our research on the area, we found that no one had ever been granted permission by the government to enter or contact a tribal group in this section of rain forest. We began praying and planning for contact with this unreached people."

"They told me about the village," you say, "but I'd like your version."

Donald's face lights with joy. He pulls off his hat and wipes his hair. "Three of us took this trek, not at all sure where we were heading. All the aerial maps showed nothing, but we knew there was a tribal group here somewhere." He points up the muddy rut. "After five hours we'd crossed twenty-seven rivers; it was pitch dark, and we got excited seeing some lights—only to find they were swarms of huge fireflies. Then finally we saw real fires, and drove into a village of the cabana-type huts of the Karitiana. Several of them had been out to visit trading posts, so a few of them knew some Portuguese. But we were the first outsiders they had seen in ten years.

"We finally understood they were having some kind of gathering in a large hut made of mud bricks. All the other huts were of palm branch. Near the door there was fish roasting over a fire, with the smoke wafting inside. Several of them insisted we enter. It was very dark, very smoky, and, well—what else could we do? With no idea what we were getting into, we ducked inside. There were candles made of gum flickering everywhere, shining off the faces of about 30 or 40 men, women, and kids.

"A man sitting in the center spoke Portuguese and said he would stop what they were doing to tell us a story. So the three of us squeezed in and sat on the ground. 'This is where we celebrate Jesus,' the man said. I know my jaw dropped and my eyes must have bugged out. I asked him to repeat it, and he told me in rough Portuguese that these 35 Karitiana were following Jesus."

At this point Donald plops has hat back on and raises his eyebrows to ask if you're finally ready to get the Jeep back in gear. "We'd better be bumping along if we're going to make it before dark. And we don't want to be out here in the dark."

You wearily climb back in. He fires the machine into its growl and yells back over his shoulder as he wrestles the steering wheel. "So he stood in the hut and gave us what amounted to a testimony. He said it was almost a year ago that he had a vision. He said Jesus came to him and took him to heaven. Somehow he knew who it was—Jesus—and knew he was seeing heaven.

"It was beautiful, filled with more people than he had ever seen. But he didn't see many Indians, and he didn't see any Karitiana. So he asked Jesus why. And he says Jesus told him, 'Because you are serving demons, not Me.' Jesus asked him his name, and he said, 'Francisco.' Then Jesus said, 'No, that is what you are called in Portuguese. What is your Karitiana name?' He replied, 'Ru-al.' Jesus said, 'Yes, I made you a Karitianan. You are worthy of the Karitiana. I made you a nation, and I want you to worship me as Karitiana.' And immediately after that he's back in his hut."

"Wow." You've got goose bumps on your arms even in the Amazon heat.

"So," yells Donald, "Ru-al has spent the last year telling everyone in the tribe what happened and what Jesus said. And so far thirty-five of them have quit worshiping spirits to follow Jesus. Amazing what God will do to call the nations to himself, eh?"

"Thirty-five doesn't seem like many," you say, and are suddenly embarrassed.

"Well, now Ru-al is training others in evangelism. The church will grow. By the way, you know how many Karitiana there are in the Amazon? In the whole world?"

You wince as the Jeep jolts you and you shake your head.

"One hundred and fifty-six." And Donald looks back and grins.

From the tiny Karitiana congregation to the massive 200,000-member churches of Buenos Aires, the evangelical church in Latin America has multiplied beyond anyone's expectations in the past 25 years.

Latin American believers have been zealous in evangelism and in starting new churches, setting "saturation church-planting" goals in most of their countries. The goal set in their regional congress in 1998 is one half million *new* congregations by 2010! Jim Montgomery of the DAWN saturation church-planting movement says that the goal "seems well within reach." Here's a glimpse of what has happened in some Latin American countries as of 2001:

New Churches	1992—2001
Brazil	20,000
Argentina	4,000
Uruguay	1,000
Chile	2,000
Peru	11,000
Colombia	3,000
Venezuela	9,000
Panama	2,000
Mexico	8,000
Dominican Republic	4,000
Costa Rica	500
El Salvador	5,000
Guatemala	12,000
Cuba	6,000

The DAWN staff add a few notes to this 2001 report:

- Recent data from a secular research company indicates that over 42% of Guatemalans are now members of evangelical churches and another 30% consider themselves to be evangelical sympathizers.
- Venezuelan believers met and prayed that their 4,900 evangelical churches would multiply to 12,000 in 10 years. They went to work, reached their goal four years ahead of time, and established a new goal of 25,000 churches by 2005!
- Uruguay, where 30% of the population claimed to be atheist in 1996, has seen that number drop to 10% while 1,000 new churches were being planted from 1996 to 1999. In the process, they reached their six-year goal in those three years!
- Cuba, after 30 years of communism, had less than 800 congregations, the same number as when the revolution started! Their goal of 5,000 new churches, mostly meeting in houses, was reached in 1998, two years ahead of their 2000 target.

There are now more Spanish speakers in the body of Christ than speakers of any other single language. All the unreached people groups of all of Latin America—mostly small, primitive tribes like the Karitiana—have been engaged by mission teams. And nearly all Latin American countries' evangelical churches are working together to send new Latin missionaries to places like West Africa, the Middle East, and Indonesia! North American pastor Leith Anderson envies that kind of progress: "South America has 50,000 new churches per year, while 60 churches per week are closing in the United States!"

Latin American Christianity is changing the face of the church: "Christianity will still be the world's largest religion for the foreseeable future, but its center is shifting from Western Europe and North America to Africa, Latin America and Asia," says Philip Jenkins in *The Next Christendom: The Coming of Global Christianity* (Oxford University Press, 2002), 2. "We are currently living through one of the transforming moments in the history of religion worldwide."

Jenkins notes that in the near future the "typical" contemporary Christian may be a woman in a Brazilian *favela* (slum) with southern beliefs and practices that will transform Christian thinking and strategy worldwide.

When the history of Latin America in the twenty-first century is written, it will be difficult for even secular historians to avoid the incredible impact of the Gospel in every one of these societies (as they have avoided the true God's impact in the history of Western civilization).

God's People Throughout History

The Roman Diognetes received the following report from an outpost in the empire in A.D. 150:

> The Christians are distinguished from other men neither by country nor language nor the customs which they observe. For they neither inhabit cities of their own nor employ a peculiar form of speech nor lead a life which is marked out by a singularity. . . . They dwell in their own countries, but simply as sojourners. As citizens, they share in all things with others and yet endure all things as if foreigners.
>
> Every foreign land is to them as their native country, and the land of their birth as a land of strangers. . . . They

are in the flesh, but they do not live after the flesh. They pass their days on earth, but they are citizens of heaven. They obey the prescribed laws of the land and at the same time surpass the laws by their lives.

They love all men and are persecuted by all. . . . They are poor yet make many rich. . . . To sum up in a word: What the soul is in the body, that is a Christian in the world.

Fulfilling their role as salt and light, voluntarily or otherwise, Christians through the ages have spread the blessing of the redemption of Christ across geographical and cultural boundaries. Since nowhere in most of our educational backgrounds is there any systematic charting of this progress of God's blessing through the centuries, let's take the time to look back briefly in the following overview of a William Carey Library article entitled "Four Men, Three Eras." (See Resources.)

We just might catch the cosmic significance of our point in history.

From Abraham to the Cross

About 2,000 years elapsed from the time God changed Abram's name to Abraham, the "Father of Nations," until the time of Christ. This span can be studied in five eras, each about 400 years in duration:

1. *The Patriarchal Period*

In roughly 400 years Abraham, Isaac, and Jacob and their families succeed and fail at various times to pass on the blessing.

2. *The Period of the Captivity*

The possible ministry of the Hebrews to their Egyptian taskmasters for a period of about 400 years is seen in the tomb of one of the Pharaohs of the time. Inscribed in his tomb is a hint that he had converted to a monotheistic religion, and written there are several phrases of Hebrew songs that later were incorporated into the Psalms. Generally, we have to conclude that the Egyptian empire rejected God's offer of blessing.

3. *The Period of the Judges*

Told they were to function as a nation of priests (Exodus 19:5–6), the children of Israel settle in a land most central to the world's trade routes. They begin to obey God's commands to rid their Promised Land of those nations that had come to their "fullness of evil," that had rejected the light of revelation. As a kingdom of priests, however, Israel itself degenerates into a helter-skelter mob in which "everyone did what was right in his own eyes" (Judges 21:25).

4. *The Period of the Kings*

In the next 400-year period God's redemptive purpose is more clearly defined as Israel's kings influence the peoples of the world in the name of the Lord God. The zenith of Israel's glory under the rule of Solomon is also the turning point of Israel's success in proclaiming abroad the excellencies of His name. The world first hears of young Solomon's fame because of the living God. Then the world hears of old Solomon's fall into idolatry, and God's reputation is defamed. A splitting of the kingdom finally results in captivity for both the northern kingdom and Judah.

5. *The Period Following the Exile*

In the roughly 400-year period between the end of the Jews' captivity and the birth of Christ, God's people learn probably more clearly than they have in centuries past that God purposed for them to bless every nation. About 100 years before Christ a biblical, devout group known as the Pharisees begin to spread God's name in earnest.

Nearly two-thirds of the captive Jews stay in Iran or Persia, and their outreach efforts are considerable. Pharisaical missionaries push north until Moses is preached in every city. As Judaism spreads south, Greek-speaking Egyptian proselytes and God-fearers help produce the Septuagint, the Greek translation of Scripture used as the Bible of the early church, and from which are taken 80% of the quotations of the Old Testament found in the New Testament.

Unfortunately, as these Jews "travel around on sea and land to make one proselyte" (Matthew 23:15), they begin to preach not so much the blessing of spiritual sonship but an outward, cultural conversion to Judaism.

The Midpoint of History

Christ's birth, ministry, death, and resurrection are central to all of history. And as we've seen, Jesus comes as a Messiah for all peoples—to the Jew first and also to all the other peoples on the planet—the Gentiles.

Five 400-year eras follow:

6. *The Roman Period* (A.D. *1 to 400*)

Partly through devotion to Christ's commission and partly through a dispersion caused by waves of persecution (Acts 8:1), believers take the Gospel across the known world.

Jesus had called His disciples the *apostles* (Luke 6:13), which literally means "sent ones." So the apostles take off! Tradition—much of it not verifiable—has it that the disciples spread their ministries east, west, south, and north:

Thomas to Iran, India
Bartholomew to India
Thaddeus to Armenia
James to Spain
Matthew to Africa, Iran
Simon the Zealot to the Middle East, Africa, and Britain
Andrew to Central Asia, the Volga area of Russia

We're fairly familiar with the missionary journeys of Paul—who was dubbed "an apostle of Gentiles" (Romans 11:13). But we might not be as familiar with some of the next generation of missionary heroes and their journeys:

Frumentius to East Africa
Denis to the Franks
Irenaeus to France
Gregory to Armenia
Patrick to Ireland
Ninian to Britain

Through about A.D. 400 God's blessing slowly invades the Roman Empire and beyond. In the early 300s Constantine as ruler of the Roman Empire moves his headquarters east into Greek territory, while a strong base of the Christian movement remains in Rome. One hundred years later, this split develops institutionally into the Eastern Orthodox and Roman families of Christendom.

The Orthodox churches settle into distinct national movements—which nonetheless send out mission teams north and east. A more international scope of Christian influence thrives and radiates out from Rome. However, Roman believers—now fashionable and no longer threatened by persecution—begin hoarding God's blessings.

As a result God sends the Gothic tribal peoples into the heart of the civilization of Rome to get what they were not sent: the blessing of the Abrahamic Covenant. They already knew of the Gospel, because earlier Rome had continuously exiled its Christian heretics into the northern and western parts of the continent.

7. *The Gothic, Celtic Period* (A.D. *400 to 800*)

The Gothic tribesmen and other European tribes such as the Celtic peoples not only receive the Gospel but produce beautifully decorated or "illuminated" manuscripts of the Bible to impress neighboring tribal chieftains.

8. *The Viking Period* (A.D. *800 to 1200*)

The Viking peoples to the north are the next to take what they have been denied. Their terrible raids on the Goths and Celts wreak massive destruction, but some of the young women they capture as slaves and wives are the messengers of the blessing of the covenant! Over a span of 250 years these ruthless peoples are gradually "held and dazzled by the effulgence of the glory of the Gospel," as Winston Churchill states in his *History of the English-Speaking Peoples* (Dodd, Mead, Rel Bxd St. edition, 1983). Overwhelmed as it were with the Gospel, they became Christian leaders of a sort in the next period.

9. *The European Period* (A.D. *1200 to 1600*)

Former ruthless European pirates lead ruthless Crusades against the Muslims in a pathetic misunderstanding of the Great Commission. Most of Europe's famous cathedrals begin to be built during a 50-year period in this era, with the intention of glorifying God—and of outdoing each other! Bible study centers earlier established by Celtic missionaries and destroyed by the Vikings are transformed by Viking descendants into larger centers of order and worship. Some of these, with a particular emphasis on scholarship and education, become the first universities.

Also, despite the atrocities of the Crusades, missionary enterprise sees a new rush as strategists such as Prince Henry the

Navigator and Christopher Columbus—both of whom are fired by devotion to Christ and to global missionary endeavor—search out new lands and new peoples.

10. *The Ends of the Earth* (A.D. *1600 to 2000)*

The period in which we find ourselves rivals all others in the extension of the Gospel. Let's look at it a little more closely.

The "Ends of the Earth" Era and God's Purpose

For nearly 200 years after the Reformation, believers, as is our pattern, focus on the top-line of the covenant. They study, analyze, and annotate the scriptural doctrines of our justification, sanctification, and glorification in Christ. The bottom-line responsibility that this blessing of salvation in Christ carries is largely left to a few zealous groups.

Great exploits occur during the 1500s, 1600s, and 1700s with the justification of "Christianizing" the world. Churches are planted in the Americas; on the fringes of Africa, south of the Sahara; across the northern reaches of Asia; and in much of southern and eastern Asia and its bordering islands. In the secularized history that has been handed down to us, most of these mission enterprises are ridiculed for their imperialistic designs and cultural abuse of the noble heathen native. A more realistic look reveals that much of this expansion does uplift the name of God among the heathen people groups of the world. For example, no secular history seems to bother examining the incredible ministry of the Danish-Halle Mission.

In 1705 the king of Denmark sends a team of German Lutheran missionaries to his colony of Tranquebar on the southeast coast of India. Of course you've never heard of Bartholomew Ziegenbalg, the godly missionary who stresses the need to study Hindu philosophy and culture to contextualize the team's church-planting efforts. He emphasizes worship—including Tamil lyrics, preaching, education, translation work, literature in the language of the people, and medical work.

And few secular historians know of the remarkable self-supporting work of the Moravian Church missionaries under the leadership of Count Zinzendorf, beginning in 1734. Purposely sent to the neglected and despised peoples of the world, the

Moravians are known for their cultural sensitivity and social interaction with unreached peoples as they patiently proclaimed the Gospel. The Moravians are renowned as well for launching a 24/7 prayer vigil for the nations—a vigil that lasted day and night for more than 100 years.

A few more experts on the history of Western civilization do take note of a wrong-side-of-the-tracks young man who in the 1790s launched what we now know as the modern mission movement.

The First Modern Mission Era (1800–1910)—The Coastlands

As a young Englishman, William Carey gets into trouble when he begins to take the Great Commission seriously. When, in the 1790s, he has the opportunity to address a group of ministers, he challenges them to give a reason why the Great Commission does not apply to them. They rebuke him, saying, "When God chooses to win the heathen, He will do it without your help or ours." He is unable to speak again on the subject, so he patiently writes his analysis, *An Enquiry Into the Obligations of Christians to Use Means for the Conversion of the Heathens.*

With a title like that, his friends are impressed enough to create a tiny mission agency, the "means" for reaching the unreached. The structure is flimsy and weak, providing only the minimal backing he needs to go to India. However, the impact of his example reverberates throughout the English-speaking world, and his little book becomes the Magna Charta of the Protestant mission movement. Messengers are sent from Europe and America to spread God's blessing to the coastlands of the earth.

Carey's heart is best seen in the covenant repeated three times yearly by those working at his mission at Serampore, India. It remains a model of Christian enterprise to this day:

1. To set an infinite value on men's souls.
2. To acquaint ourselves with the snares that hold the minds of people.
3. To abstain from whatever deepens India's prejudice against the Gospel.
4. To watch for every chance of doing the people good.

5. To preach Christ crucified as the grand means of conversions.
6. To esteem and treat the Indians always as our equals.
7. To guard and build up the hosts that may be gathered.
8. To cultivate their spiritual gifts, ever pressing upon them their missionary obligation since only Indians can win India for Christ.
9. To labor increasingly in biblical translation.
10. To be instant in the nurture of personal religion.
11. To give ourselves without reserve to the Cause, not counting even the clothes we wear our own.

Carey's great watchword: "Expect great things from God; attempt great things for God!" His little book, in combination with the Great Awakening in America in the early 1800s, quickens vision and changes lives on both sides of the Atlantic.

In America, five college students, stirred by Carey's book, meet to pray for God's direction for their lives. This unobtrusive prayer meeting, later known as the "Haystack Prayer Meeting," results in an American "means"—the American Board of Commissioners for Foreign Missions. Even more important, their example starts a student mission movement that becomes the forerunner of other student movements in missions to this day.

Carey's influence leads some women in Boston to form women's missionary prayer groups, a trend that leads to women becoming the main custodians of mission knowledge and motivation. After some years women begin to go to the field as single missionaries. Finally, by 1865, unmarried American women establish women's mission boards that, like Roman Catholic women's orders, only send out single women as missionaries and are run entirely by single women at home.

In the First Era of modern missions progress on the field is painfully and agonizingly slow. Missionary after missionary succumbs to fever, especially in West Africa. Early missionaries are well aware that they are probably going to their death. Out of thirty-five who go to Ghana between 1835 and 1870, only two live more than two years. Yet the Gospel takes root and grows.

Where the Gospel goes to the coastlands of the world the results are often amazing. As a result, in 1865, missionaries from the Hawaiian Islands (one of the earliest fields) begin to go home. They believe the job is done. With their withdrawal the First Era in missions begins to decline. But another is about to begin.

The Second Modern Mission Era (1865–1980)—The Inland Frontiers

Hudson Taylor, also a young man, is considered impertinent because he tries to start a new mission organization. With much trepidation he does so in 1865, even though that's the year missionaries are being brought home from Hawaii. It takes 20 years for other missions to begin to join Taylor in his special emphasis—the untouched *inland* frontiers.

One reason the Second Era begins slowly is that many people are confused. On the one hand, missionaries are coming home: "Isn't the job done?" On the other hand, there are millions of unsaved individuals: "It's hopeless to open new fields!" There are already many missions in existence. Why more? "Why go to the interior if you haven't finished the job on the coast?"

Finally, in the late 1880s, existing agencies begin to retool for new fields, and a rash of new mission agencies are born with the new inland emphasis: the Sudan Interior Mission, African Inland Mission, Regions Beyond Missionary Union, and others.

As in the early stage of the First Era, as things begin to move, God brings forth a student movement. This one is more massive than before—the Student Volunteer Movement for Foreign Missions. In the 1880s and 1890s the number of college students is considerably less—only about 3% of what it will be in the 1990s. Even so, the Student Volunteer Movement nets 100,000 volunteers who give their lives to missions. And of these, 20,000 actually go overseas. The other 80,000 stay home as senders.

By 1925 the largest mission movement in history is in full swing. Second Era missionaries have planted churches in 1,000 new places, mainly "inland." By the 1940s the strength of these churches leads both national leaders and missionaries to assume that all additional frontiers could simply be mopped up by the ordinary evangelism of the churches scattered throughout the world. More and more people wonder if, in fact, missionaries are still needed. Once more, as in 1865, it seems logical to send missionaries home from many areas of the world.

In 1967 the total number of career missionaries from America begins to decline. Why? Christians have been led to believe that all necessary beachheads have been established. By 1967 over 90% of all missionaries from North America are working with strong national churches that have been in existence for some time.

The facts, however, are not that simple. Unnoticed by most everyone, another era in missions has begun.

The Third Modern Mission Era (1935-)—To the Ends of the Earth

This era is begun by two other young men, both Student Volunteers of the Second Era: W. Cameron Townsend and Donald A. McGavran.

Cameron Townsend is in such a hurry to get to Central America that he doesn't bother to finish college. In Guatemala, as in all other mission fields, there is plenty for the missionary to do working with established national churches. But Townsend is alert enough to notice that the majority of the population does not speak Spanish. As he moves from village to village, trying to distribute Scriptures in the Spanish language, he begins to realize along with certain other missionaries that Spanish evangelism will never reach all the people of Guatemala. He is further convinced of this when an Indian asks him, "If your God is so smart, why can't he speak our language?"

In response, Townsend launches Wycliffe Bible Translators, dedicated to reaching these new frontiers, the overlooked pockets of tribal people groups.

At the very same time Townsend and his friends are struggling with the challenge of groups isolated by language, missionary Donald McGavran is beginning to see the seriousness of India's amazing social barriers.

Starting in the 1970s others (often disciples of McGavran) begin to realize even more clearly just how many unreached people groups exist in our world. They point out that many of these pockets of peoples have been completely overlooked by missionaries and national churches alike. These groups are defined by ethnic or sociological traits to be people so different from the cultural traditions of any existing church that mission (rather than evangelism) strategies are necessary for the planting of indigenous churches among them. Which brings us up to today—this we'll examine in the next chapter.

A New Worldview

Perhaps the history reviewed here bumps against the way you've always looked at things. For instance, most Christians in the Western Hemisphere are dumbfounded to read the personal journals of Christopher Columbus, which reveal so clearly his heart of love for God and his commitment to spread the Gospel.

And if you have not been a student of the Bible, you might be feeling something of the same shock from our Bible studies thus far: How could I have missed this almost monotonous repetition of God's unchangeable purpose for the nations, the peoples whom the Jews call *the Gentiles*! Why haven't I seen before the importance of God's name being lifted up, of our role as priests? How can it be that even in familiar passages, the obvious theme of God's heart for every people group has been overlooked in my years of hearing and reading those portions in church or in Bible classes?

If so, what you're feeling is the basic uneasiness of a shifting worldview. A "worldview" is simply the way we look at things: what we do, what we value, and what we think is true and real. And perhaps your worldview so far in life has been tinted by cultural Christianity, which emphasizes personal top-line blessing and de-emphasizes the reality of Satan's counter-kingdom.

Cultural professor Norman Geisler explains our worldviews like a pair of colored eyeglasses. Our worldviews color everything we look at. And since most of us have been wearing the same set of glasses since birth, as we grew up in a culture, it's pretty hard to set those glasses aside and suddenly pick up a different pair to look at the world.

● Greetings reflect worldviews. In France, good friends kiss each other—two or three times, depending on the relationship. In Mexico, friends embrace. In most people groups in India, greeters put their hands together and bow slightly; they're thus able to greet many people at once and don't pass on germs by touching. And to say hello, the Siriano of

South America simply spit on each other's chest!

- The English sit and sleep on raised surfaces because their cultural glasses tell them that floors are dirty. To many oriental peoples, floors are clean; so they, of course, remove their shoes at the door and sit and sleep on mats on the floor. To a Korean or Japanese, having a guest who's wearing shoes walk onto the floor is like a guest in England stomping across the sofa or bed with his shoes on!

- Paul Hiebert, professor of anthropology at Fuller School of World Mission, tells the anecdote: A mixed-culture group was eating at an Indian restaurant when a Canadian asked, "Do Indians really eat with their fingers?" "Yes, we do," the Indian replied. "But we look at it differently. You see, we wash our hands carefully. And besides, they have never been in anyone else's mouth. But look at these spoons and forks. Think about how many other people have already had them inside their mouths!"

In Latin, English, Sanskrit, Greek, and several other languages, one meaning for the phrase *to see* is "to know." That is, the way we look at life through our cultural worldview "glasses" is the way we *know* it to be.

This fact has all sorts of implications if you're a person ministering within another culture. But it also has implications if you've begun to catch a vision of God's heart—of what He has been doing throughout biblical and post-biblical history.

Cross-cultural workers know that a change of behavior doesn't change a person's heart, that imposing Western culture on a person has nothing to do with a changed worldview. "As [a person] thinks within himself, so he is. He says to you, 'Eat and drink!' But his heart is not with you" (Proverbs 23:7). Making a people into a capitalistic, well-clothed parody of Western civilization has never been God's design for blessing the nations with the Gospel. His blessing comes by giving them new hearts in Christ—new, true ways of looking at the world.

Plotting Your Worldview

Think through this simplified worldview diagram.

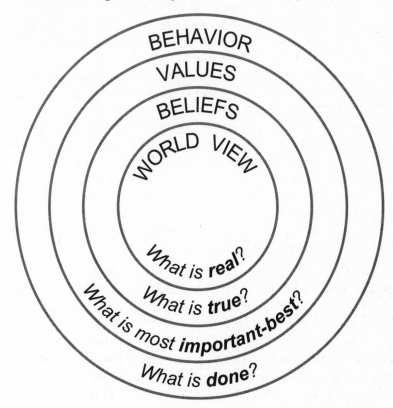

The core of our worldview is the way we think in our hearts about what is real. This reality is formed by what we've decided about questions such as:

- Who or what is in charge of life?
- What is this Person or this force doing?
- Where do I fit in?

Unfortunately, what's very real to a person might not be true. A life built on a false reality will always be off-center.

What we feel is real affects what we believe. What we believe affects our attitudes of what is good and best. And attitudes finally affect our behavior. Try to visualize the kind of worldview shift that might occur in your life as you catch the vision!

The typical Christian worldview is something like this:

What is real? Well, God is real. He is on the throne, although a lot goes on in the world that He allows to happen because of man's evil choices. I fit into this scheme of things as His child who doesn't have a lot to say about cosmic events.

What do I believe? Among other things, I believe the Bible. I believe that God chose the Jews to finally bring forth the Messiah so He could start the church so I could become a Christian—which means I'm different from the world, but if I live true to God I'll have a good life with His blessing. I also believe things are going from bad to worse, and when they get really out-of-hand, God will give up on humanity, Jesus will return, and I'll go to heaven.

What do I think is best? I think being a good Christian is extremely important—living a clean, godly life, reading the Bible, praying, witnessing, giving money to the church and missions, and attending church services.

What is my behavior like? I try to do the things I know are important; but I don't do them as regularly as I should or would like to. I attend lots of meetings. And I'm basically trying to have the best life I can until Jesus comes back for me.

Now, this worldview may sound commendable, but is it based on what is true?

Let's look at a worldview based on the Scriptures we've studied:

What is real? God is minutely in charge of everything, even to the extent of using Satan and man's wrath to fit into His unchangeable purpose of blessing His people in order to bless every people on earth. I fit into a very specific role in that plan.

What do I believe? Among other things, such as the doctrines of the faith, I believe God has been orchestrating His specific plan for all of history. I believe that everything that happens fits into His unchangeable purpose. And I believe there is a time coming when He will finish His plan. I believe that time is soon, and I believe my growing sense of vision of His plan is not a coincidence: I believe He wants to use me now in some significant way.

What do I think is best? Fitting into that plan. Seeking first

His kingdom. Using all the disciplines of biblical Christianity to point in the direction of that purpose. It is important for me to maintain good health, cultivate good relationships, keep my finances in order so that I can give as much as possible to the cause of Christ, walk in the paths of righteousness for His name's sake, and develop all my skills and spiritual gifts for my part in the big picture. It's also crucial to me to very carefully and very gratefully count and enjoy God's blessings on my life. I want to understand what He's done and is doing in me that needs to be turned into blessings for others—in my own people and other people groups. I want to pray against the enemy strongholds so that God's kingdom can come on earth as it is in heaven, and pray that God would thrust forth laborers into His harvest. I am intent on uniting with other believers in this cosmic battle against satanic forces. I'm alert to sin in my own life, wanting to be clean and pure, not just to be "good," but because my daily standing before God has huge implications *beyond my life,* I want to be a vessel fit for God's use in His plans! All of this is extremely important, because God is carrying out His purpose through us, His people!

What is my behavior like? It looks like typical Christian behavior, only a little more radical. I've never prayed so much in my life since I understand better the privilege and responsibility of the priesthood of the believer; I become angry over Satan's control over a certain unreached people group and I refuse through prayer to let Satan have his way over them. I'm getting together with Christians who mean business, because I know better than to tackle the strongholds of Satan by myself. And we don't just talk fluff—even Christian fluff; we all know it's not all about us! I'm also studying the Bible and the world like never before, because I've realized how little I know about the whole picture. I'm not having so much trouble succumbing to temptation, because saying yes to God's powerful purpose makes it easier to say no to the distractions of sin. I actually take time to evaluate everything I do to pull it into captivity to obedience to Christ and His great cause, and I "houseclean" my life activities regularly. I evaluate what I have and do according to the fact that it has a purpose far beyond making my own life comfortable. I find I don't do much in the way of trying to "keep up with the Joneses"; who cares about such small ambitions any-more? I'm feeling less of a need to escape, so I watch less TV and spend less money.

I'm beginning to think and feel and act as if I don't quite belong here anymore.

Whether God is pressing us back into the Word, urging us to rethink some of our history lessons, or asking if a worldview shift is needed, He wants us to know what He is doing and to join Him in it. Today.

For Further Thought

1. Memorize Proverbs 23:7: "As he thinks within himself, so he is." Consider your own worldview. How would you fully answer:

   - Who or what is in charge of life?
   - What is this Person or this force doing?
   - Where do I fit in?

2. Give yourself a history exam. Review this chapter's sketch of global history. Then jot down each of the 10 epochs of roughly 400 years each.
3. With a friend, discuss the "typical Christian worldview" and a "worldview based on Scripture." Explain to your friend the rationale behind each factor in the scriptural worldview.

2020 VISION

THE FINAL TASK:

It Can Be Done, It Must Be Done!

NORTH AMERICA

• Colorado Springs

Colorado Springs, U.S.A. You panic as Dan Scribner shoves the cordless microphone into your hand. Yes, you're foolishly sitting near the podium on the front row of the auditorium—the dreaded spot when it comes to being involuntarily volunteered. You simply want to observe, but he insists, "Please? Just hold the mic for whoever gives a report? If you let them hold it, they'll go on forever. You know mission fanatics and their stories!"

"Sure." You come out of your daze as he announces to the crowd of hundreds: "Now, who had a breakthrough in what God is doing today?"

You run up and down the aisle, around to the front, back to the very back row, down the main aisle again—and hold the microphone as dozens of people stand to eagerly add their anecdote:

- "I belong to the Gideons organization, and our volunteers now hand out more than one million copies of Scripture *every week* in 175 countries. And there are hundreds of other organizations distributing God's Word besides us!"
- "Ninety percent of the world can now listen to Christian radio in a language they know!"
- "Giving to foreign missions by Christians in Canada from '96 to '99 increased by more than 35%!"
- "In the southern section of Sudan, about 5% of the population was Christian in 1960. Today, after decades of horrible warfare and persecution, the figure is close to 70% Christian!"
- "One hundred years ago Korea was said to be 'impenetrable by the Gospel.' Today almost one-third of the entire population are believers in Christ! There are 7,000 churches in Seoul alone!" You pull the microphone away to head for the next report, but the Korea fanatic grabs the mic and almost shouts, "And Korea now has 12,000 missionaries in 156 countries!"
- "From the Islamic Revolution in 1979 up until 2003—sorry, these are the latest figures we have—more Iranians came to faith in Christ than in the previous 1,000 years combined. There were 300 believers in Iran in '79. Now that number has multiplied 100 times to more than 30,000!"
- "When William Carey went to India in 1793, for every true believer in the world, there were 49 people who would say they were not Christians. Now for every true believer in the world, there are just seven who say they're not Christians!"
- "An average of 3,500 new churches are now opening every week around the world!"
- "North America now has 575,000 churches! That's a church for every 537 Canadians and Americans. But there's a need for more ethnic churches, since it's estimated that in

the year 2050 the U.S. will be 50% Hispanic."

- You almost drop the microphone as a pale researcher stops you and intones, "Yes, but of all those churches in North America, 60 are closing every week!"

- "Just to remind ourselves of what we're doing here—" The old man you've run up to grasps the mic right over your own hand. He's obviously a preacher as he holds out his battered old Bible like a silver serving tray. "Isaiah 12, verses 4 and 5: '"Give thanks to the LORD, call on His name. Make known His deeds among the peoples; make them remember that His name is exalted." Praise the LORD in song, for He has done excellent things; let this be known throughout the earth.' We're obeying these commands!"

- The next person is a teenage girl with her Bible open as well. "I was thinking of a passage too. It's like you older people telling us younger about what God is doing around the world. All we usually hear is bad news, and it's scary. Well, Psalm 145: 4–6 says (I've got the NIV): 'One generation will commend your works to another; they will tell of your mighty acts. They will speak of the glorious splendor of your majesty, and I will meditate on your wonderful works. They will tell of the power of your awesome works, and I will proclaim your great deeds.'"

- "Hi, I'm just in from Paris, where in August this year 500 Chinese pastors got together to strategize how their congregations in Europe can coordinate with the 100,000 missionaries the house churches of China plan to send in the Back to Jerusalem movement. Heard of it?" You nod and run to the next person. This is getting to be quite a workout.

- An elderly woman struggles to stand, but you gesture for her to remain seated. She too grasps the mic around your hand: "The largest gathering of humans in history was at a prayer meeting I attended in Yoido Plaza in—" The whole crowd seems to turn toward the Korea fanatic who just spoke moments ago, and dozens of voices yell, "Seoul, Korea!" "Yes," she continues, "for prayer on that Saturday morning, 2,700,000 came to pray!"

- "Over a three-month period in Mombassa, Kenya, nearly

60,000 Muslims came to faith in Jesus Christ as a result of the healing of a little girl in a mosque—a healing in the name of Jesus!"

- "As of 2004 Christians worldwide put in 192 billion man-hours of evangelism every year!"

- "In Nagaland, in northeast India, 95% of the state's three million people confess Jesus Christ as Lord! They've vowed to send out 10,000 new missionaries to India and beyond!"

- "Just completed a new tally. Nearly three billion people— almost half the world's population—have seen the *Jesus* film! We've got 2,144 projection teams constantly out there now, showing the film in 228 countries in 863 languages—languages that 90% of the world's peoples understand. And since the film's release in '79 we've seen 197,298,327 indicate decisions for Christ as a result!"

- "Puerto Rico now has the highest number of evangelical believers per square mile of any place in the world! Of the 3.5 million population, one million are evangelicals—with 7,000 churches, 10,000 pastors, nine Christian TV stations, thirteen Christian radio stations, 130 Christian schools, and 350 Christian community service organizations. And about one thousand young Puerto Ricans are training to go as missionaries to the Muslim world; they call themselves *Las Catacumbas* (The Ones From the Catacombs)!"

You jog across the front, perspiring now, past Dan. "This is inspiring, but I'm about worn out."

"Of course." He grins. "It's a big world out there, and we have a big God!"

"Thanks," you oddly respond, and run to the next man waving to you.

- "We got a fax from Hong Kong describing a team of very elderly 'Bible women' in China. Wherever they go, they tell the Christians that it's 'Gospel Month.' Every believer is to share her or his faith that month until at least one person says yes to Christ. So where there were 50,000 believers in an area, at the end of the month there are 100,000! No wonder China is the fastest-growing part of the body of Christ!"

Mercifully, Dan says into his microphone, "Okay, I think that's all we have time for. Thank you." You stagger back to him and hand over your cordless mic. He says to you, "Thanks," but hangs on to your sleeve. "But we still need you."

You wipe the sweat off your cheeks and stand, embarrassed, next to Dan in front of this mob of maybe 1,000 mission zealots. More than 40 major mission agencies have located in Colorado Springs in the past decade. Pooling their research and, like today, their anecdotal breakthroughs, enriches their collaboration.

"Thanks for these reminders of Habakkuk 1:5, 'Look among the nations! Observe! Be astonished! Wonder! Because I am doing something in your days—you would not believe if you were told.' I'm Dan Scribner with the Joshua Project, and welcome! For a demonstration of what the world looks like today . . . in a very, very general way; I see you researchers out there. Yes, this is going to be ballpark percentages, okay?" A few of the IT engineering types frown, but Dan braves on: "You can do this in your church or fellowship group. But I'll need nine more victims—er, volunteers. Yes, volunteers. Just stand where you are."

And slowly across the crowd, nine stand. You're the only one awkwardly standing at the front. Dan turns to you.

"Now, we had wanted to invite the entire world's population, but the fire marshal nixed the idea. So these ten will have to represent the whole lot of us. Here, friends, is one of every ten persons in the world. Ten percent." He glances at the research corner. "Actually, more like eleven percent, but we're not quibbling today, are we? For every ten people in the world today, one—" He gestures as if you're the prize on a game show. "One is a committed Christian! Yes!"

The crowd claps; you smile and bow.

"Look saintly, now," Dan tells you. "Then we have two . . ." He waves to the nearest two standing. "Nominal Christians. Don't look too saintly, okay?" They and the group chuckle. "Now, statistically, two of every ten people in the world say they know Jesus Christ as Savior and Lord, and say they share their faith. Okay, now you four. Yes, wave. Okay, four of every ten in the world are . . ." Dramatic pause. "Pagans! That's right! They may be here in a Christian meeting, but these folks are obviously . . . pagan! No, actually, these are the four of every ten who simply will tell you that they are not Christians. They've heard of Christ, but they have not decided to follow Him. Yet. Got it so far? For every ten people in the world, there is one . . . ?" He gestures to you. You try to look saintly, and the crowd yells, "Committed Christian!"

Then he points toward the two nearest you. "And two . . . ?"

"Nominal Christians."

He nods toward the four. "And four . . . ?"

"Pagans!"

"In cultures where there are committed Christians, but so far they've said no to Christ. Always good to think of these folks—forty percent of the world—as 'pre-Christians.' Notice how they're near nominal and committed Christians, in cultures that have strong churches. All right! Now, how about those three suspects back there?"

Everyone turns to look at the final three standing toward the back.

"These are the . . . serious . . . pagans!" People chuckle, then stop. Dan gets serious: "They don't know Christ, and they're in cultures where God's character is not demonstrated, where there aren't any churches, or the churches there aren't strong enough to evangelize their own people. These are people without God and without hope, and they've never even heard of Jesus Christ!"

The TV game show atmosphere has faded, and everyone sobers. These three out of every ten humans are the captives, those chained in spiritual darkness, held prisoners in Satan's counter-kingdom. Pretty hard to joke about the plight of these living, breathing men, women, and children who share in our humanity.

"If this is what our world looks like, what needs to happen here? Talk amongst yourselves! One committed Christian. Two nominal Christians. Four pre-Christians—non-Christians in cultures that have a Gospel witness. And finally three non-Christians in people groups that are unreached, untouched by the Good News. I'll give you sixty seconds: What needs to happen in our world?"

Dan turns to you while the auditorium buzzes with discussion. "Well?"

You stutter a little. "You want me to answer that?"

"What needs to happen?"

"Uh—"

He breaks in with a shout: "Thirty seconds!"

You're flustered. "I guess the committed Christian—"

"That's you, right?"

"Yeah."

Suddenly he shouts a countdown to the crowd. "Ten seconds, nine, eight, seven . . ."

You're lucky; you don't have to come up with a strategy. You can't think that fast after the blitz of input you've had lately about what God is doing, about what He's been doing all along in Scripture.

Dan says, "Okay! Let's have some ideas!" And for the next few minutes this eager, smart audience comes up with three tactics. Dan summarizes: "So what is it called when nominal Christians are challenged to quit their lowdown ways and live up to their commitment to Christ? Now, some of these nominals aren't really believers at all; that's not for us to judge. But some are, and when challenged to genuinely live for Christ, they'll slap their foreheads, repent, and move into the committed category, right? What's it called when nominal Christians recommit their lives to Christ?"

Several in the crowd call out, "Revival!"

Dan says, "Okay, and you came up with another answer to what needs to happen in our world. What's it called when Christians share their faith with the non-Christians in their own culture?"

More yell out, "Evangelism!"

"Yes! And what is it called to demonstrate the name of Christ, to take the blessing of redemption in Christ to the nations who have never heard?"

Everyone seems to say it together, including you: "Missions."

Dan concludes the fun but amazingly clear demonstration. "So encourage your fellow believers that if God is stirring their hearts for revival in churches among twenty percent of humanity, this is their day! And if God has burdened them with compassion for forty percent of mankind, the non-Christians in cultures that have a Gospel witness, this is the day for evangelism! And, if God is saying something to them, rattling their comfort zones about what He is doing to proclaim the excellencies of His name among thirty percent of the world in unreached people groups?"

The crowd responds: "This is the day!"

Dan concludes, "And fortunately, revival, evangelism, and missions can all happen at once since today there are probably seven hundred million committed Christians. Let's help each other fit into God's strategy for what needs to happen in our world!"

Later, long after the last stragglers exit the auditorium, you suggest to Dan, "Maybe there's a fourth thing that needs to happen. As in—sort of a catalyst for revival and evangelism and missions in a church. It has to start with somebody, so it's got to be the committed Christian."

Dan winds up a microphone cord. "And that's you, right?"

"Well—I think so," you say. "Something about the committed Christian having a vision beyond himself, his own Christian walk. Getting serious about prayer. Getting a better understanding of God's worldview—"

"That's what this book is about, right?"

You're suddenly disoriented. "Well, yeah . . ."

Looking the World Over

What's the state of the world? Even general information about God's *harvest field*—"the field is the world" (Matthew 13:38)—can help clarify your part in God's *harvest force*. A Proverb puts it: "What a shame—yes, how stupid!—to decide before knowing the facts!" (Proverbs 18:13 TLB).

A memorable categorization of the harvest field is used by many researchers and churches:

- World C: The 10% of the world population who are committed Christians plus the 20% who are nominal Christians comprise World C.
- World B: The 40% of our global population who are non-Christians living in people groups with churches are World B.
- World A: The 30% of the world that makes up the popu-

lations of unreached peoples are World A.

The people of World A reside mostly in a rectangular box stretching from West Africa to the eastern edge of Asia between the ten- and forty-degree north latitudes. This area has come to be called "The 10/40 Window."

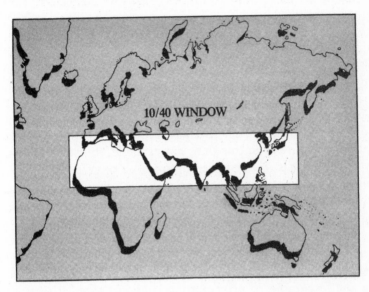

- More than 95% of the world's unreached peoples live in this area.
- The 10/40 Window outlines the heartlands of the world's major non-Christian religions: Islam, Hinduism, Buddhism, Shinto, Confucianism, etc.
- Two-thirds of the world's population lives in this region.
- About 80% of the poorest of the world's poor live in this window, enduring humanity's lowest standards of living.
- Most of the political countries in this window restrict the proclamation of the Gospel.

A very general breakdown of the unreached peoples in World A includes three religions—Islam, Hinduism, Buddhism—and two cultural groups: Chinese and Tribal. Remember, of course, that there are other groups of unreached peoples that don't fit into these neat, general categories. Look in the

Resources section at the back of this book for suggestions on how to learn more about the categorization of unreached groups.

But we need to think more specifically about these unreached peoples if we're to catch a clear vision of God's plan in our day.

People-Group Thinking

God deals very personally and very intimately with individuals—but almost always in the context of groups: in families, in cities, in generations, in people groups.

A common view is that the biblical term *nations* refers to countries. Political boundaries and geography are key in this outlook. The accurate view is that *nations* refers to peoples; cultural distinctions are key in this view. For example, the political country of Sudan has, counting sub-groups, more than 500 distinct cultural groups or *nations* within its borders. The political country of India comprises 2,329 *nations*. Some political countries are homogenous in their ethnicity, and so the majority people group is called by the name of the political country itself: the German people of Germany, the Russian people of Russia, Koreans of South or North Korea, etc. Unfortunately, this often confuses our understanding of people-group thinking when it comes to the biblical concept of *nations*.

When Jesus commissioned us New Testament believers to "disciple the nations" (Matthew 28:19), He used the Greek term *ethne,* from which we get the English word *ethnic.*

In the era between the Testaments the Jews began referring to all the other ethnic groups as "the Gentiles." References in Scripture to the *Gentiles* don't primarily pinpoint non-Jewish individuals so much as all the nations other than the Jewish nation.

A reading of sample biblical passages—even without commentary—can alert us to God's heart for the nations:

Genesis 12:1–3
Genesis 18:18
Genesis 22:17–18
Genesis 26:4
Genesis 28:14

2 Chronicles 6:32–33
Psalm 67:1–2, 7
Malachi 1:11
Matthew 24:14
Matthew 28:19–20
Luke 24:44–47
Romans 1:5
Galatians 3:8
Revelation 5:9

Definitions used by many nation-focused world-watchers can be helpful in understanding our point in the history of God's global purpose:

What defines a people group? There are several fine definitions used by missiologists, anthropologists, and researchers. Of course, these varying definitions lead to varying numbers of reached and unreached people groups. For example, if a group lives in several political countries—such as the Baluch do—is each group to be considered distinct because they live on opposite sides of an imaginary line or wire fence called a border? And what about sub-groups that have differing dialects of spoken language but identical written languages? Yes, the numbers can get complicated! But a basic definition that fits most needs is that espoused by the mission bulletin *Mission Frontiers.* As the MF Web site (*www.MissionFrontiers.org*) explains:

> A people group is a significantly large ethnic or sociological grouping of individuals who perceive themselves to have a common affinity for one another. For evangelistic purposes, it is the largest group within which the Gospel can spread as a church-planting movement without encountering barriers of understanding or acceptance.

● There are perhaps 16,200 people groups on the planet according to this definition. Just 50 of these groups comprise half of the world's total population.

What is a reached people? A nation is missiologically considered "reached" when it has a strong enough church to evangelize its own people. This in no way suggests that all the individuals within a people group have become believers or have even yet encountered the claims of Jesus Christ; that's the goal of evangelism.

A people group is considered "reached" if it has a viable, indigenous, self-reproducing church movement in its midst. A reached people has strong churches led by its own people using their own heart-language. These churches are actively evangelizing their people and are reproducing daughter churches.

- About 10,000 people groups on the planet qualify as "reached." These people groups live mostly in the 171 (of the total 234) political countries of the world, which are Christian-majority countries (with committed as well as nominal Christian adherents).

What is an unreached people? An unreached or "least-reached" people has no church movement. If there are any Christians, they are less than 2% of the population.

A people group is "unreached" if there is no indigenous community of believing Christians with adequate numbers and resources to evangelize its own people without outside (cross-cultural) assistance.

- Today there are perhaps 6,200 remaining unreached peoples on earth.

A majority of these unreached peoples lives within the 10/40 Window. But 1,410 of them live outside that restrictive window, and nearly all of these are represented by immigrants in democratic countries where it is legal to proclaim the Gospel.

About 56% (3,538) of these groups are small, with a population under 10,000. Another 1,519 groups have a 50,000+ population, which renders them more accessible in terms of language, literacy, openness to outsiders, existing networks with other groups, etc. For example, the largest least-reached/unreached people in the world are the Japanese, whose population is 120 million.

We're told to "let the nations be glad and sing for joy" (Psalm 67:4). There are at least 6,200 nations who know nothing of the mandate "Praise the LORD, all nations; laud Him, all peoples!" (Psalm 117:1).

Strategic Thinking

God has been pushing through the sweep of history to finish His clear, unchangeable purpose on earth: To bless His people so that every people may be blessed. And it's time we gear up more strategically to join His big plans for our own era.

A common view is to focus on counting numbers of individuals who have come to Christ or who have not received Christ. This view often suggests that in order to complete the Great Commission we must spell out the Gospel to every individual on earth. Frankly, it's a pretty hopeless outlook! This view sometimes uses the term *unreached people* to apply to any individuals who are not Christians and says that "we're all missionaries"— meaning we're all to share Christ. But this view confuses personal evangelism with missions, and it renders the Great Commission an unrealistic ideal rather than a practical, clear plan.

The strategic view of God's purpose focuses first on sending foreign believers—missionaries—into each unreached people group. These outsiders, ministering cross-culturally, nurture new believers into sharing their faith. Slowly a fellowship of believers grows into a church. The church, again with foreign discipling, begins to evangelize its expanding networks of friends, family, neighbors—and new churches spring forth. In most of the world this natural, spontaneous multiplication of churches is unencumbered by the devilish three Bs of institutional Christendom: Budgets, Buildings, and "Big shots"!

As sufficient presence and resources are developed within the indigenous church movement, the foreigners shift into a partnership role, serving if and as needed to see the entire people group—individual by individual—reached by the claims of Christ as believers model all that Christ commanded. Meanwhile, the new churches send out their own missionaries to repeat this cross-cultural process in another people group!

This strategic view accentuates the clarity of God's commission: The blessing of redemption is to be offered to every nation. It is then the responsibility of that nation's church movement to stand up for God's character in its own culture, to proclaim His salvation person by person.

All Around the World

In simple, and sometimes spectacular, ways God is carrying out His strategic plan of calling out a people to bear His name—to bless the nations. What does this look like in today's progress of the kingdom?

Massive Proclamation

- Hundreds of translation ministries are working hard to provide the written Word in the languages of every nation. Wycliffe Bible Translators, for example, states on its Web site that "380 million people in over 3,000 language groups still wait for the Good News in their own languages. They have waited long enough!" Fifteen hundred translation projects are in progress currently, and the organization vows: "By the year 2025, together with partners worldwide, we aim to see a Bible translation program begun in all the remaining languages that need one."

- Of the planet's 7,291 languages (as of 2004, with an average of 64 languages disappearing every year as new generations learn more marketable languages), 3,572 have some form of God's Word—in print, in Gospel recordings, in TV or radio broadcasts, or on film. These formats of the Gospel are heard or read and understood by 90% of the globe's population.

- Sat–7, a satellite television station, digitally broadcasts the Good News across the entire Arab world 24 hours a day. One viewer wrote: "We are about 140 families, and we live in a remote area of Syria where there are no churches yet. The programs are like medicine to our sickness!"

- Working with radio ministries like HCJB, TWR, and FEBC, Galcom distributes radios pre-tuned and set on Christian broadcasts. In one Estonian prison some 200 prisoners who had access to Galcom radios accepted Christ and began making plans for baptism. In the first three years of TransWorld Radio's Bulgarian Gypsy broadcasts, seven churches were planted as Gypsy families gathered around their radios to Christian programming, the only broadcasts in their Romani language. Recently

Swedish radio ministry IBRA saw a church form in Say—a major Muslim university city in Niger, Africa—as a result of its Christian broadcasts. Pray for this new congregation, one of thousands of quiet "radio churches" in restricted areas around the world.

An Expanding Harvest Force

- Mass media sometimes breaks up hard ground; then, on-site cross-cultural workers put a face to the Gospel. God is sending out a massive harvest force. For example, American IMB mission executive Jerry Rankin reports record numbers of career missionaries being appointed year after year; as of 2003 there were 5,403 cross-cultural personnel working among 1,317 people groups. Collectively they saw more than one-half million baptisms of new believers and 16,721 new churches established in 2003 alone! Rankin says, "What excites me is that God is moving as never before. Is it any wonder that He is stirring the hearts of His people to respond to His call?"

- A pastor from Palermo, Sicily, felt led to move to unchurched Lampedusa, an Italian island close to Tunisia, where Muslim immigrants from North Africa often are stranded as their boats break up trying to sail to Europe. The pastor started a new church, which within months grew to 25 members—just one of the hundreds of thousands of unsung heroes who daily go "out for the sake of the Name" (3 John 7)!

- Churches in people groups that only recently were mission fields are now part of the mission force. In the Czech Republic churches began sending out missionaries in the mid-'90s to Chechnya and the Balkans. When asked why those particular areas, church leaders responded, "Because we can drive there!" Now Czech missionaries are going farther: Pastor Milan Szturc has led his church to cooperate with six other local churches—from across denominational lines—to send a Czech family as new missionaries to Indonesia.

- Today's missionaries are just as likely to be Nigerian or

Brazilian as American or European. Thousands of Two-Thirds-World missionaries are going to countries where Western missionaries aren't welcome. They live modestly with very little support. Over an eight-year period, Lily of the Valley Church in Costa Rica sent out 21 new missionaries to Mali, Senegal, and Mauritania. The small congregation supports its mission force through sacrifice: Pastor Gilbert Rowe has given up his own salary, workers volunteer at the church's Antioch Garage, and other members run a bakery. The fellowship commits 80% of its funds to prepare future missionaries and support those already sent.

● A recent Latin Missionary Consultation convened in—where else?—Savanger, Norway! Its purpose? To plan new inroads for Latin American missionary work in the Muslim communities of Europe.

● Global thinkers are strategizing creative approaches to bless the nations. For example, the September 2004 Forum for World Evangelization Conference in Thailand featured a track on "Business As Mission." The 10/40 Window contains 80% of the world's poor. These peoples have the world's fastest population growth, with 30–80% of them unemployed. The forum generated plans to mobilize Christian entrepreneurs to start profitable businesses in areas like the 10/40 Window, pointing out: "Over the next twenty years more than three billion people will enter societies where there are few churches and no jobs. What should the response of the church be to such a challenge?"

● "Welcomers"—cross-cultural missionaries in democratic countries who welcome international students, refugees, immigrants, and diplomats—are realizing the impact of their ministries among unreached peoples. One Canadian welcomer meets refugee families from Kosovo as they arrive in Canada. He helps them find jobs and furniture for their apartments. Then he invites them to a meal and tells them, "I am your pastor, like your *imam*." "How can that be?" they respond. "We're Muslim and you're a Christian." "I just am," he says without explanation, and begins to lead them through the Messianic Psalms. Over the two years of this "welcoming" ministry, two extended family groups of

Kosovar Albanians have come to faith in Christ!

- God, of course, has His eye on His Register of the Peoples (Psalm 87:6). And sometimes He himself initiates a breakthrough into an unreached people. Kingdom Ministries' Florian Bärtsch works among the more than 60 hardened unreached peoples of the Caucasus region between the Black and Caspian Seas. No one had heard of any believers among one of these groups, the Kabardians. Then in February 2004 Florian learned of God's intervention in a young Kabardian's life. The man was in prison. In desperation, he slit his wrists. Just as he was losing consciousness, Jesus appeared to him and said, "I am giving you a second chance." Miraculously, the young man later awoke and saw his blood on the floor of his cell. But his wounds were completely healed. During the rest of his jail term, he studiously read a Russian Bible. After his release from prison, he told his story among Kabardians wherever he went, and he introduced people to Christ, who are forming house churches—the first churches among the Kabardians in all of history!

Spontaneous Multiplication

- What happens when foreign cross-cultural workers establish churches in a people group? The natural result is that the church grows like wildfire! In mainland China, sub-Saharan Africa, and Latin America, there is now a Pentecost every hour—more than 3,000 newcomers join the body of Christ every hour of every day, 24/7!

- Churches are growing with new believers in places most of us have never even heard of: Nearly 1,000 born-again Inuit from across the Arctic filled the Iqaluit, Nunavut, curling rink for a week of raucous, joyful worship in the summer of 2004. For the first time Inuit from Greenland joined others of the Inuit people for their festive annual Bible conference. How much of what God is doing occurs outside your Christian networks—in places you've never heard of such as Iqaluit, Nunavut?

- Protestant missionaries first arrived in the Philippines in 1899. Seventy-five years later, in 1974, there were 5,000

Bible-believing churches in the country. In that year 75 Filipino church leaders met to strategize for growth. They knew their 35,000 *barangays* (villages or city neighborhoods) would grow to 50,000 by 2000. So by faith they set a goal of seeing a total of 50,000 churches by the year 2000. Emphasizing in every denomination and in every church the priority of personal evangelism that results in whole new fellowships, the 25-year project covered a difficult period in Filipino history. They endured chaos during the overthrow of the dictator Marcos, several major earthquakes, typhoons, floods, volcanic eruptions, rebellions by Muslim extremists, and economic uncertainties. The results 25 years later?

They exceeded their goal! At a celebration party, representatives of 28 denominations, 44 parachurch ministries and independent churches announced, "There are now 51,625 Filipino local churches and 3,125 cross-cultural missionaries trained and deployed"! And, of course, the group set new goals for 2010: "To identify in repentance with the sins of our people, pray for revival, desire the outpouring of His Spirit upon our lives, people, and churches, and to live in obedience to the Word of the Lord." Then they got specific: To trust God for *50,000 more churches* sending out 3,000 more missionaries by 2010! Christian Filipinos fill many of the housekeeping, nanny, and manual labor jobs of many societies in the 10/40 Window; so the group additionally vowed to send out "tens of thousands of tentmakers to the world"! DAWN Movement staffers who helped facilitate the phenomenal 25-year project commented, "If the Great Commission is to be completed in our time, this is the way to do it!"

God is creatively offering His blessing to the nations as He builds His church. And the gates of hell cannot prevail against it!

The Final Frontiers

Today God has packed more humans on planet Earth than ever before in history. Since He values human souls more than anything else in His creation, it's safe to expect that He is about to do something spectacular in our era. And it will be according to His plan to bless His people so the nations can be blessed:

> God be gracious to us and bless us,
> And cause His face to shine upon us—
> That Your way may be known on the earth,
> Your salvation among all nations.
> God blesses us,
> That all the ends of the earth may fear Him.
> (Psalm 67:1–2, 7)

Think through the following chart of how our task of discipling the nations compares to what the early church disciples faced.

In Genesis 10 God described the beginning of the nations; 70 are listed. Over the centuries these groups scattered, split, and diversified. At the time of Christ, some missiological historians suggest, there may have been as many as 60,000 small people groups on the face of the earth—with its total population of just two million! These were the *ethne,* the groups the Jews called the *Gentiles.* On the first Day of Pentecost, there was only one nation—the Jewish nation—that had a core of believers who would be strong enough to evangelize their own people. That left 59,999 unreached people groups! We can only imagine the disciples' discomfort as Jesus told them to make disciples of *every* nation! The task seemed even more improbable when, after His crucifixion, Jesus told His followers to "wait for what the Father had promised" in Jerusalem (Acts 1:4), and out of all the multitudes who once followed Him, only 120 people obeyed.

ERA	HARVEST FORCE	HARVEST FIELD	RATIO	PRINCIPLES
A.D. 33	Among thousands of followers of Christ, 120 committed, true believers in one Upper-Room "congregation"	59,999 Unreached People Groups	One congregation to reach 59,999 people groups: A ratio of 1:59,999!	God empowers a church that is: 1. Obedient (Acts 1:4) 2. Unified (Acts 2:1) 3. Strategic (Acts 2:5) 4. Multiplying (Acts 2:39)

Yet the obedient, unified team of disciples followed God's strategy as He *brought* some "from every nation under heaven" (Acts 2:5) to Jerusalem for that unique Day of Pentecost! As they multiplied the proclamation of their message not only among their own but also among those who were "afar off," this outnumbered little band soon "turned the world upside down" (Acts 17:6 NKJV).

Now picture our era's privilege and responsibility to fit into God's historic plan. We do have a few advantages over the early disciples. We have made incredible advances in travel, communication, language, cultural education, methodologies, and resources compared to what the early church had. And there are more of us—many, many more (even though these estimates are very general). For illustration's sake, if we grouped today's 700 million committed believers into congregations of 80 each (the average size of a church globally) we would have 8,800,000 congregations of committed Christians! And, obviously, we have far fewer unreached peoples to disciple:

ERA	HARVEST FORCE	HARVEST FIELD	RATIO	PRINCIPLES
A.D. 2005–2010	Among more than 2.6 billion followers of Christ, about 700 million committed, true believers (11% of world population) in about 8.8 million congregations	6,200 remaining unreached people groups	4 million congregations to reach 6,200 peoples. A ratio of 1,420 congregations (with 113,600 committed Christians) for every one remaining unreached people!	God still empowers a church that is: 1. Obedient (Acts 1:4) 2. Unified (Acts 2:1) 3. Strategic (Acts 2:5) 4. Multiplying (Acts 2:39)

What if the body of Christ in the twenty-first century moved carefully in obedience for the sake of His name? What if 113,600 committed believers and their churches could join together in unity to focus on one unreached people? What if we followed God-given strategies, if we focused on multiplying our message and our lives? Isn't it a little obvious—even with these generalizations—that God could once again turn our world upside down for the cause of the kingdom?

At the end of time Christ will be exalted with the song "You were killed, and your blood has ransomed people for God from every tribe and language and people and nation" (Revelation 5:9 NLT). The task of reaching the remaining nations with this news is only a matter of when and through whom.

It Can Be Done, It Must Be Done!

Imagine. It's a September morning in 1913. We're standing on a rise over the ocean in a balmy tropical breeze. We're looking south to the white waves of the Pacific crunching onto the smooth sand of Panama. We turn and look back to the unbelievable sacrifice of years and lives and funds represented in the huge ditch carved through the ridges and jungles from the Caribbean forty miles to the north. You remember how French engineer

Ferdinand de Lesseps set out in 1872 to finish the task of a canal across the Isthmus of Panama. More than 20,000 men died from tropical diseases and infected injuries before de Lesseps gave up just seven years later.

Now you've extended what the French began, and you're within sight of completing the entire project. We're standing on a one-hundred-yard stretch of solid rock that still remains to be removed to complete the Panama Canal, one of the greatest engineering achievements in human history. Forty miles completed, one hundred yards to go.

Chief engineer George Goethals strides up the slight rise and nods, "It's all here. We've got the dynamite to do it. The workers are ready. We've gone over the calculations again and again. This rock is tough. Might be the toughest obstacle this crew has faced. But we figure we can cut our way through to the Pacific in about two days. We're ready. What do you say?"

As long as we're imagining, let's imagine you're the boss on this monumental project. What do you say?

When you see the end in sight on a huge project it's not too tough to shout, "Let's finish the job!"

Now, in the twenty-first century, the completion of the greatest project in human history is within sight. It's determined that the church has the necessary information, the necessary resources, and the necessary manpower to send church-planting teams to every remaining unreached people group on earth—to at least *begin* the process of discipling in each nation.

You think of the words of D. L. Moody, an evangelist in the 1890s: "It can be done. It must be done!"

But blasting through the remaining tasks of this cosmic enterprise will not be easy; there will be blood, sweat, tears, and more body counts. Remember the twofold problem we humans are embroiled in? Satan and his entire kingdom of darkness hate the idea that the Great Commission, one day, will be finished.

For Further Thought

1. Think through again and memorize the details of Matthew 28:18–20.
2. Plot out your own scenario of how a church can be planted

in a hypothetical people group. (Or strategize about an actual unreached people; see Resources section at the back of this book for more information.) Actually diagram your scheme. Then after some serious prayer, mark *your* place in that scenario. Of course, no man-made plan, yours included, is adequate for what God is doing. But thinking through the steps will help clarify your own strategic role in the general pattern of God's great purpose!

3. Spend a day this week in prayer and fasting concerning what God wants for you in the coming year or how you can fine-tune your personal ministry within the cause.

4. Tell a few friends about your scenario of how an entire unreached people might be reached. It's guaranteed to be a lively discussion!

CHAPTER 12

GLOBAL WARFARE:

The Battle Belongs to the Lord

Northwest Nigeria. You're sitting on a warm, round rock at the edge of the village well, mopping your face, terrified.

The dry, cracked buzz of cicadas in the scrub oaks around the dusty village square is the only sound. Villagers stand in a silent circle of heat waves around a white-robed warrior. His muscled arms poise the sword high over a kneeling young man who now gently places his right arm across the wood stump in front of him.

The young man's wife and sister stand trembling just behind him as he kneels in the dust. Around the inside of the circle, the children cringe in silence, fingers in mouths. You sit paralyzed, feeling nauseated.

The Hausa warrior shouts slowly in his language, then in

English for your benefit: "This pastor Selchun was carrying a Christian Bible!" He glares eye-to-eye around the circle of breathless villagers, then at you. "This is the punishment for all infidels!" And he grunts as the sword slashes through the hot air to thump through the wrist and into the wood stump.

Pastor Selchun chokes in pain, but without blinking an eye, he raises his left hand and begins to sing. You recognize the melody: "He is Lord, He is Lord. He has risen from the dead and He is Lord."

The dusty villagers stare wide-eyed in silence. Even the Hausa warrior seems struck dumb. Your heart is in your throat as the kneeling, bloody young man sings, "Every knee shall bow, every tongue confess that Jesus Christ is Lord!"

Pastor Selchun is only one of the victims of the mounting do-or-die spiritual battle for this planet. At the time of this true incident, almost 60,000 Christians were homeless in Pastor Selchun's area of Nigeria, driven from their homes by violent mobs. About 300 Christians had been murdered over a three-month period, some of them burned alive in their meeting houses as more than 100 churches were torched.

It's always unnerving to realize that the Greek word for *witness*—"You shall be My witnesses" (Acts 1:8)—is *martys,* "martyr." So it's not surprising that the global body of Christ is taking some hard knocks. The findings of the best research in the world on Christian martyrdom is shocking:

Christian martyrs killed since A.D 33	69,420,000
Martyrs in the 20th century	45,400,000
Average annual martyrs killed since 1950	278,000 per year
Countries in which Christians are now being martyred	50
Martyrs killed in the year 2000	160,000*

Nigeria is one of those countries in which believer after believer has given his or her life for Christ. In 1960 Nigeria, the most populous country in Africa, was 50% Muslim, 40% animist, and 10% Christian. Today it's 50% Muslim and 50% Christian—thus the flare-ups, the tension, the conflicts, and the

*Source: World Christian Trends 2001. Barrett & Johnson, William Carey Library.

martyrdom of those killed simply because they're Christians.

But it's not just through religious martyrdom that Satan is striking out against believers. They are also often caught up in the wholesale slaughter of the innocents in rebel wars, in purges that are themselves satanic weapons. When the plane carrying Rwandan President Juvénal Habyarimana was shot down on April 6, 1994, the genocide of an estimated one million people commenced—a demonic massacre that shocked the world. Hundreds of thousands of believers were slaughtered in that insane genocide. As in other horrific events in our recent history, the claw marks of the enemy—who is intent on stealing, killing, and destroying (John 10:10) is obvious.

The continent of Africa sparkles here and there with revivals, with more than 20,000 coming to Christ daily and more than 50% of sub-Saharan Africans claiming that they follow Jesus and share their faith. So the god of this world rages and seeks to destroy wherever he can. He and his world-system of principalities, powers, and rulers of darkness are the spiritual force behind ethnic wars as well as other horrible new weapons in Africa—such as AIDS:

> An estimated 25 million adults and children are living with HIV in sub-Saharan Africa, and an estimated twelve million African children have been orphaned by HIV/AIDS. During 2003 as many as 2.2 million people in this region died from AIDS.

Adults (age 15 & up) living with HIV/AIDS in the worst-hit countries of sub-Saharan Africa:

Country	Adults	Adult Rate %	Orphans due to AIDS
Botswana	330,000	37.3	120,000
Dem. Rep. Congo	1,000,000	4.2	770,000
Ethiopia	1,400,000	4.4	720,000
Kenya	1,100,000	6.7	650,000
Lesotho	300,000	28.9	100,000
Malawi	810,000	14.2	500,000

Mozambique	1,200,000	12.2	470,000
Namibia	200,000	21.3	57,000
Nigeria	3,300,000	5.4	1,800,000
South Africa	5,100,000	21.5	1,100,000
Swaziland	200,000	38.8	65,000
Tanzania	1,500,000	8.8	980,000
Zambia	830,000	16.5	630,000
Zimbabwe	1,600,000	24.6	980,000
All Sub-Saharan Countries	23,100,000	7.5	12,100,000

Year-End 2003 Estimates: UNAIDS

Twelve million AIDS orphans—and that's just in sub-Saharan Africa. Notice the 3,300,000 infected in Nigeria and the nearly two million children without parents due to AIDS deaths in that one country. Try not to think about the suffering of the AIDS victims in other regions of the world. And the millions more children abandoned because of this raging pandemic. Try to pretend that God doesn't notice—as many of us in the church seem to feel AIDS is not our business. Pretend that this slaughter isn't a horrible, intentional new tactic of the enemy of men's souls—Satan and his world-system.

Satan seems to get his tentacles around every group in which his usurped kingdom stands in jeopardy, where the possible light of the glorious gospel of Christ might shine into the hearts of those enslaved in his darkness. Humans are only pawns in his competition with God, and he uses them and destroys them without a thought.

And you think you're going to stand in his way?

The exciting, global-scale push to bring the Gospel to every *ethne* isn't just a simple matter of reaching human beings. All the extraordinary plans to evangelize the world also threaten the kingdom of darkness. The prince of this world is going to make sure the final task of completing the Great Commission will not be easy.

This is not a game.

The Catch

Through our study, you might have wondered: If the biblical mandate is so clear, if the big picture of what God is doing in our world today is so exciting, if the 6,300 remaining people groups can actually be reached with the Gospel, if millions are dying without God and without hope, why isn't all of Christendom buzzing with the news that we can finish the task? What's the catch?

Here's the easy answer: There is a cost.

That's the catch. Obedience costs. Real discipleship costs. The price? Giving up our small personal agendas that detract from God's global cause. Forsaking our comfortable lives, giving up claims of ownership to security. The challenge today is exactly like the one that faced Francis Xavier. Five hundred years ago he dreamed of returning to Paris from his mission work in India, China, and Japan. Why? So he could walk up and down the streets shouting to the students of Paris: "Give up your small ambitions!"

Obedience means giving up ownership of our personal agendas. Obedience means shifting our expectations to becoming a blessing instead of merely being blessed. The price of being a part of God's historic global purpose is losing your life for His sake. Denying your old self. Taking up your cross—which in Jesus' day meant you wouldn't need to worry much about things that most people worry about. Taking up your cross is a picture of you standing with a noose around your neck; you've put yourself at God's disposal so thoroughly that you have nothing left to lose.

An old parable often told among believers across Africa pictures just how tough it is to give up our own ambitions:

> One day Jesus asked each of His disciples to pick up a stone to carry for Him. John took the biggest one he could find, while Peter picked a small one. Jesus took them up to the top of a mountain and commanded the stones to be bread. Each was allowed to eat the bread he found in his hands, but of course Peter did not have much to eat at all. John then shared some of his with Peter.
>
> On another occasion Jesus again asked the disciples to carry stones for Him. This time, instead of leading them to

a mountaintop, he took them to the River Jordan. "Cast the stones into the river," was His command this time. The disciples looked at one another in bewilderment. What could be the point? They had lugged those stones all this way (And you know who picked the big one this time, don't you?). Throw them into the river? Why? But they obeyed.

Jesus turned to them and said, "For whom did you carry the stone?"

Sometimes the Christian disciplines of denial of self, facing afflictions, solid prayer, and study in the Word seem pointless. What's the purpose of denying self and taking up your cross daily? A nicer life? Success, so things will work out well in our lives? Or is discipleship a discipline with purpose—to become a closer follower of Christ to "make disciples of all *ethne*"?

Jesus didn't pander to our self-seeking instincts:

"He who loves father or mother more than Me is not worthy of Me; and he who loves son or daughter more than Me is not worthy of Me. And he who does not take his cross and follow after Me is not worthy of Me. He who has found his life will lose it, and he who has lost his life for My sake will find it" (Matthew 10:37–39).

Looking at him, Jesus felt a love for him and said to him, "One thing you lack: go and sell all you possess and give to the poor, and you will have treasure in heaven; and come, follow Me" (Mark 10:21).

Another also said, "I will follow You, Lord; but first permit me to say good-bye to those at home." But Jesus said to him, "No one, after putting his hand to the plow and looking back, is fit for the kingdom of God" (Luke 9:61–62).

"So then, none of you can be My disciple who does not give up all his own possessions" (Luke 14:33).

There are many fine expositions and Bible studies published on these and other "hard" passages concerning the disciplines of true discipleship. But even the most earnest attempts to soften these stringencies of following Jesus must conclude that the price of selling yourself as a bondslave for the Master's use can be high. In the Bible a life sold out to His purpose is compared to the rigors of the lifestyle of an athlete in training, a hard-working farmer, and a combat soldier (2 Timothy 2:3–10).

Perhaps too many of us modern-day Christians have been led to believe that Christianity is supposed to be nice—respectable, predictable, reasonable, and smooth. We are deceived into thinking that being the people of God means lots of meetings and lots of blessings. Many of us believers who are living in relatively safe, democratic countries have grown to believe that if we love Jesus we won't get hurt. If we do get hurt in life, or our children do, it must be that we lack faith. But believers in oppressive countries know that partaking in the sufferings of Christ isn't a metaphor; pain in the spiritual war zone of earthly life is very, very real: "Rejoice that you participate in the sufferings of Christ" (1 Peter 4:13 NIV); "Indeed, all who desire to live godly in Christ Jesus will be persecuted" (2 Timothy 3:12).

God says that Satan's world-system is out to get us: "If the world [Satan's world-system] hates you, keep in mind that it hated me first" (John 15:18 NIV). He suggests that humans dedicated to the satanic counter-kingdom can destroy us. For example:

A king will arise,
Insolent and skilled in intrigue.
His power will be mighty, but not by his own power,
And he will destroy to an extraordinary degree
And prosper and perform his will;
He will destroy mighty men and the holy people.
(Daniel 8:23–24)

Why isn't all of Christendom humming with the excitement of finishing the task? Because it's not exactly going to be a breeze. It never has been. Since it's global war there are going to be casualties and body counts. Living out your part in God's great purpose won't be easy.

Prisoners of Darkness

Africa is a continent where people by people, area by area, God is releasing captives from the stranglehold of Satan's principalities, powers, and rulers of darkness. And it may be a good place to pause and visualize again the interwoven threads of

God's twofold plan, one that incorporates the abolishing of Satan's counter-kingdom and at the same time accomplishing the redemption of humans held captive in the bonds of darkness.

We're not only naïve, we're also unbiblical if we think that evangelism is a practical matter of persuasively explaining salvation. Unbelieving individuals and unbelieving societies don't see it, don't hear it, and can't understand it if their minds are still blinded by spiritual darkness.

Imagine. As a six-year-old you were kidnapped into one of the hundreds of fanatic rebel armies crisscrossing the African continent—perhaps the ironically named "Lord's Resistance Army." You tote supplies, are forced to walk ahead through minefields, and learn to fire your own AK–47 Kalashnikov. This rag-tag rebel army has been thoroughly defeated by the country's army and is destined to be finally exterminated by the government's vastly superior force. But you don't know this; your fellow rebels simply fight; they don't understand the politics and don't follow the news.

A famous rebel commander directs the activities in your base camp. You're afraid of him, knowing his background as a ruthless murderer. You once witnessed his brutal cruelty when a villager refused to work. The leader pulled out a Glock machine pistol and simply shot him in the head. The commander is unquestionably the boss around here, and you go along with all the others in following his leadership. It's as if there is no choice.

You can continue the allegory, but the point is clear: An officially defeated despot can still rule over a group of people who allow him to rule over them.

How does he do this? He lies.

Satan is the "father of lies" (John 8:44). He deceives the nations (Revelation 20:3, 8). He is the "serpent of old who is called the devil and Satan, who deceives the whole world; he was thrown down to the earth, and his angels were thrown down with him" (Revelation 12:9). Imagine that his lies are like a line tossed from the spiritual heavenlies dimension down to a group of humans—a people group. If they grab on to the lie they secure that line and drive a stake at that point: *This is what we believe.* The lie might simply be the Deceiver saying, "I'm in charge here. There is no God." Or, "A woman is only a piece of property." Or, "You are the most important people on earth." The more lies that a people accepts, the thicker the dark threads, the lines that interweave to gradually cover them in darkness:

> On this mountain the LORD Almighty
> will prepare a feast of rich food for all peoples,
> a banquet of aged wine—
> the best of meats and the finest of wines.
> On this mountain he will destroy
> the shroud that enfolds all peoples,
> the sheet that covers all nations.
> (Isaiah 25:6–7 NIV)

Other translations describe this covering as a *veil*, a *death-shroud*. A people accepts a lie, teaches the lie to its children, then lives out the lie. And lie after lie after lie—which they agree to believe—they are covered in darkness. The lies reinforce every other lie, and the web of false thinking, false beliefs, sin and its generational consequences, gets thicker and thicker through the centuries. The false beliefs become strongholds, solid spiritual walls around that people's hearts and minds.

Satan and his false kingdom still rule over peoples who allow them to be their ruler. They have been officially defeated; on the cross Christ "disarmed the rulers and authorities, He made a public display of them, having triumphed over them" (Colossians 2:15). But God's timetable still pinpoints a future date when Christ "hands over the kingdom to the God and Father, when He has abolished all rule and all authority and power" (1 Corinthians 15:24). The die is cast: Satan as "the ruler of this world will be cast out" (John 12:31).

In the meantime Satan's diabolical world-system is busily deceiving the nations with lies. The world-system's specialty is propaganda and delusion. Today at least 6,300 people groups virtually believe they have no choice but to be subject to Satan's rule. The dark god of this world-system has blinded their minds (2 Corinthians 4:4) so they as a people can't see the light of the Gospel even if it were beamed brilliantly from space! The individuals within these people groups are captive to the power that rules them in darkness.

Fortunately, in the satanic spiritual walls around these people groups there are gates; let's call them the "gates of hell." Gates, where the authorities sat in ancient times, are meant to be opened . . . for the King of Glory:

Lift up your heads, O gates,
And be lifted up, O ancient doors,
That the King of glory may come in!
(Psalm 24:7)

God's people, the church, can take the offensive: Jesus said, "This is the rock on which I will put together my church, a church so expansive with energy that not even the gates of hell will be able to keep it out" (Matthew 16:18 THE MESSAGE).

We are, as God's "royal priesthood, called . . . out of darkness into His marvelous light" (1 Peter 2:9). Isn't it only fair that we intercede in our priestly role to see God break through the gates of hell and pull down the strongholds? God says to His people:

I have called you in righteousness . . .
As a light to the nations,
To open blind eyes,
To bring out prisoners from the dungeon
And those who dwell in darkness from the prison.
I am the Lord; that is My name.
(Isaiah 42:6–8)

Soldier Priests

Jesus spoke of the principle that you can't "enter the strong man's house and carry off his property"—to rescue the perishing—"unless [you] first bind the strong man." The wording in the original Greek here emphasizes the article *the*. Jesus is referring to a particular strong man—Satan. Then, Jesus said, you can "plunder his house" (Matthew 12:29). Now, Satan and his organized hierarchy of principalities, powers, and rulers of darkness are *spiritual* entities. They are creatures of "the heavenlies." How can we, with our feet on the ground, "bind the strong man" to bring out prisoners from Satan's dungeon? How can we tear apart that death shroud that keeps an entire people in spiritual darkness?

201

Christ entrusted to God's people the incredible priestly duty of agreeing together to bind and loose: "Whatever you shall bind on earth shall be bound in heaven; and whatever you loose on earth shall be loosed in heaven" (Matthew 18:18; see also Matthew 16:18–19). Our struggle, Paul clearly insists, is not against humans—flesh and blood—but against the powers that manipulate them in Satan's world system: "Our struggle is . . . against the rulers, against the powers, against the world forces of this darkness, against the spiritual forces of wickedness in the heavenly places" (Ephesians 6:12).

What do we do in this struggle? "Though we walk in the flesh, we do not war according to the flesh, for the weapons of our warfare are not of the flesh, but divinely powerful for the destruction of fortresses" or strongholds—even if the structure of those strongholds is buttressed on nothing more tangible than world-system lies, false ideas: "speculations and every lofty thing raised up against the knowledge of God" (2 Corinthians 10:3–5). (The 70-year domination of millions under Communism should tell us what effect a satanically backed idea can have.)

Agreeing in prayer is, of course, a primary weapon:

- *Pray to pull down satanic fortresses over unreached people groups* (2 Corinthians 10:3–4). Go ahead, vent your anger in prayer against the powers of evil that hold 6,300 people groups under the cruel, ugly, destructive god of this world. It's not fair! Life under the domain of darkness is not just. Innocent people are caught in its trap. If we accept their condition as "just the way it is," we've given in to the world-system's status quo. Someone has suggested that prayer is the ultimate rebellion against the status quo. It's all right to be angry; refuse to accept the injustice, the destitution, and the preventable illnesses. As the poor widow persisted in presenting her case because of the injustice done her (Luke 18:1–8), persist in prayer until victories are won in the heavenlies.

Even if you can't work up your own anger against Satan's domain, take God's side in the matter. God's wrath against evil never cools. Intercede, refusing to accept the way things are in the world. That is the very nature of spiritual warfare in prayer.

● *Pray for the saints involved in reaching the captives.* Listen to Paul's clear plea for prayer that closes his warning to put on the whole armor of God:

> "With all prayer and petition pray at all times in the Spirit, and with this in view, be on the alert with all perseverance and petition for all the saints, and pray on my behalf, that utterance may be given to me in the opening of my mouth, to make known with boldness the mystery of the gospel" (Ephesians 6:18–19).

● *Pray for new laborers.* You've been looking at the fields that are ripened for harvest. Now "beseech the Lord of the harvest to send out workers into His harvest" (Matthew 9:38). Remember that the term for "send out" is more correctly translated "thrust out." It is the same word used when Jesus thrust out the money changers from the temple's court of the Gentiles, the same New Testament term used for casting out spirits. Being "thrust out" may even be a bit uncomfortable for those God sends into His harvest. But pray!

Another weapon of our warfare in the heavenlies is a strong testimony—one that means business, that says we are willing to go to extremes in obedience to Christ. The blood-bought authority with which Christ directs His harvest of making disciples among all the nations (Matthew 28:18–19) empowers our testimony to break the grip of Satan. John writes:

> Then I heard a loud voice in heaven, saying, "Now the salvation, and the power, and the kingdom of our God and the authority of His Christ have come, for the accuser [the meaning of Satan's name] of our brethren has been thrown down. . . . And they overcame him because of the blood of the Lamb and because of the word of their testimony, and they did not love their life even when faced with death" (Revelation 12:10–11).

Though a testimony may seem a vague weapon in spiritual warfare, accept it as fact: A surrendered life cleansed by the blood of Christ can break through Satan's barriers to bring light to the captives!

Another weapon used to defeat Satan's minions is a combination of faithful prayer and fasting; Christ said that some powerful spirits of the counter-kingdom don't give up their control "except by prayer and fasting" (see Matthew 17:14–21).

A powerful weapon is the sword of the Spirit, which is the Word of God (Ephesians 6:17). It is an offensive weapon to be used against the forces of the evil one. Jesus used it skillfully in the incident recorded in Matthew 4:1–11. But it is important to note that abiding in the Word isn't only head knowledge of Scripture. No mere intellectual compilation of the Bible's information daunts Satan—he can quote Scripture too, and answer trivia questions about the Bible probably better than you can! The weapon that defeats the deception of the enemy is truth; and Christ said that the Word is truth (John 17:17). Let the Word of Christ *dwell* in you richly.

There are more weapons in our spiritual arsenal. And there are many good studies on the topic. (See the Resources section in the back of the book for information.) But before you tackle serious spiritual battling for the sake of God's unchangeable purpose, be forewarned. Spiritual warfare is not a new fad in a Christian sub-culture; it is not a game.

Satan and his world-system organization are powerful. Perhaps you thought spiritual warfare amounts to battling the awesome hordes of hell over your temptation to watch too much TV or eat an extra eclair. Fighting against our flesh and denying self is one thing. Warring against the satanic counter-kingdom on behalf of an unreached people group is more like going into battle with 10,000 soldiers against a king who has 20,000. Our meager resources are no match for his (see Luke 14:28–32). This diabolical army knows man's weaknesses; Satan's representatives can actually "wear down the saints of the Highest One" (Daniel 7:25)!

Prayer advocate Peter Wagner warns: "Dealing with territorial spirits is major league warfare and should not be undertaken casually. I know few who have the necessary expertise, and if you do not know what you are doing, Satan will eat you for breakfast." (Spiritual Warfare Conference, Pasadena, CA, Oct. 1997)

He suggests two examples in a 1989 issue of *Evangelical Missions Quarterly*: Wilson Awasu, one of Wagner's students, reported that in Ghana a pastor, over the protests of his congregation, oversaw the cutting down of a tree that had been enshrined by satanists. As the last branch was sawed off the pastor suddenly collapsed on the spot and died. As another pastor demolished a fetish shrine he inexplicably suffered a stroke. Wagner's advice? Never underestimate the power of the enemy.

Paul wrote constantly of afflictions, hardships, hunger, beatings, and imprisonment. As God's people are gathered together into one from among the nations (John 11:52), as we make known "the riches of the glory of this mystery among the Gentiles" (Colossians 1:27), we need to be aware that some individuals will be called upon to "fill up what is lacking in Christ's afflictions" (Colossians 1:24). Paul urged that "no one . . . be disturbed by these afflictions; for you yourselves know that we have been destined for this" (1 Thessalonians 3:3).

Paul knew the reality of the enemy. With the possible exception of the book of Philemon, all of Paul's writings refer to Satan and his plans to destroy believers' priestly ministry of grace and apostleship. God's command through Paul to "take up the full armor of God so that you will be able to resist in the evil day" (Ephesians 6:13) suggests we need to be prepared for something a bit more dangerous than the annual church business meeting.

Is it any wonder that not too many of the more than two billion who call themselves Christians are signing up to finish the task, to follow to the death God's clear mandate of discipling the nations?

Hell Hath Fury

Satan delights when believers cheat, lie, swear, swagger in drunkenness, hate each other, get jealous, and spread rumors, because their sin defames God's great name. But these sinful activities, shameful as they are, have little effect on the state of Satan's counter-kingdom. He can allow plenty more believers to attend church regularly, clean up their lives, and even pray for one another's illnesses. In fact, he can let a few Christians' relatives and neighbors come to Christ without worrying about his evil forces being thwarted in the least.

However, there is one thing Satan is ultimately concerned about: himself. He knows Scripture better than any believer, and he knows he will eventually be relegated with his demonic hordes to the Lake of Fire (Revelation 20:10). The only thing he can do meanwhile is to "buy time."

One major factor in Scripture spells out the timing of his final doom. So if there is a key biblical passage Satan is ultimately concerned about, it is a simple verse in the book of Matthew: (One mission thinker suggests that if there is a boardroom in hell, this is the verse inscribed over the podium.)

> This gospel of the kingdom shall be preached in the whole world for a witness to all the nations, and then the end will come. (Matthew 24:14)

An end to Satan's reign is a personal threat to him. And regardless of your views on future events, this verse clearly equates the end with the proclamation of the Gospel as a witness to all the nations, to every people group on the face of the earth.

As we thrust forth laborers into the harvest, as we endure hardship as good soldiers for the cause of Christ, as we gird ourselves to remain standing in spiritual battle, people group after people group will be reached. The countdown has begun. Satan's dominion over the peoples is, in the present progressive words of John, "passing away" (1 John 2:17).

The closer we get to that time when the last unreached people group will witness the proclamation of the Gospel in its own culture, in its own language, the closer Satan comes to the end. Note that foreigners mass-broadcasting the Gospel isn't what signals "the end." Nor is it even a few from every people turning to Christ. The verse describes an indigenous demonstration, a testimony, a witness illustrating the kingship of God in every culture. Jesus commanded us to *make disciples* of every nation, not to simply get a few individuals to listen to our preaching.

Still, "knowing that he has only a short time," the devil rages (Revelation 12:12).

The final task of reaching every people on the face of the globe will not be painless. We have an adversary. But God is looking for a few good men and women to fight the good fight, to overcome. "He who has an ear, let him hear what the Spirit says to the churches" (Revelation 3:22).

Storming the Gates

So the battle of Christendom is to confirm God's claim on people group after people group, to pull down the satanic strongholds that keep them prisoners of darkness. It is a progressive war, with battles won and lost in the heavenlies that result in casualties, blood, sweat, and tears on the ground. But the gates of hell will not stand against the advance of Christ's church (Matthew 16:18). The world system that holds 6,300 people groups in darkness is "passing away."

We are winning.

As we fulfill our priestly duties of intercession for the nations, individuals in the presently unreached people groups will begin to respond to the Gospel proclaimed by cross-cultural missionaries. In fact, God makes it clear as He "registers the peoples" that even among people groups that cumulatively reject Him some individuals will be saved. God says that "this one and that one" from even the Babylonians and the Philistines were born in Zion—born again. These individuals will live side by side with believers representing every people and tongue in our hometown, the eternal city of the New Jerusalem (Psalm 87:4–6).

As more and more individuals within a people group come to Christ the satanic strongholds are weakened. An indigenous church is established; then more churches spring up in a church movement that can evangelize the entire people group and demonstrate the Gospel of the kingdom to that culture. Then whoever calls upon the name of the Lord will be saved.

But how can they call on a God they don't believe in?

And how can they believe in God if they don't hear about Him?

And how can they hear about Him without a proclaimer of the excellencies of this God who calls us out of darkness into His marvelous light?

And how can anyone proclaim this message to peoples among whom Christ is not named—except they be sent?

Well?

For Further Thought

1. Take a full week to memorize Ephesians 6:10–19 and meditate on the necessity of being equipped for spiritual warfare.

2. Locate on a map the African countries listed with the most serious AIDS crises, and intercede. Pray *for* the affected individuals, and pray *against* the enemy that is destroying their lives, their families, and their people.

3. Contact your mission agency to find the name of an unreached group in one of those countries. Or, on the Web, look up the various countries' unreached people groups at *www.joshuaproject.net/index.php* and ask God to direct you to intercede for a particular unreached people. Pray specifically over each item you learn about that people. And pray for the Lord of the Harvest to "thrust out" laborers into that group!

4. Present your findings about that unreached people to a prayer group who will join you in the disciplines of spiritual battle *for* that people and *against* the strongholds over them.

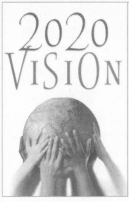

CHAPTER 13

RUNNING WITH THE VISION:

Action Steps and Resources

Mopti, Mali. You know there will be Bozos in heaven. No, not those bozos. The Bozos, an unreached people in Mali. A fishing people living along the Niger and Bani Rivers. You can't help but chuckle, knowing that at this very moment back in your home church they're praying for you in this crucial first-time meeting. And they're praying for the Bozos!

Because you read some book about what God is doing globally, your church thought you knew something about how to negotiate with the elders of an unreached tribal group. You had flown in to what, after all your quantum leaps across the world, still feels like the uttermost part of the earth. You landed in

Ouagadougou, in Burkina Faso. You thought you were to meet with the leaders of the Bobo people—the disdained nation in Mali renowned for their love of dog meat. The animal-control people of the country. But then a phone call clarified it: Not the Bobos, the Bozos! Of course. You'd driven north into Mali, to the town of Mopti—almost to Timbuktu. To meet with Bozos.

You clear your throat as you sit down for tea with the elder political leaders of the town. In Mali French, they ask, "We do not worship your Christian God. Why should we allow you to stir up our citizens about Jesus Christ?"

Through your translator, you say, "In my hometown, the Christians have declared our city to be a 'hunger-free zone.' They're seeing to it that no one in our city goes hungry ever again. Would you like to see that happen here in Mopti? In my neighborhood, Christians have developed a job training center for young people. Would you like several of these across the towns of the Bozos? All the Christians in my town are helping solve problems of alcoholism and lack of child care for working mothers. They're helping people learn to read, and are caring for the elderly.

"There are Christian businessmen and women in my home city who have been sharpening their skills for years as they helped bless my town. Some have said they will come to Mali to train your young people in starting new businesses. Others will help you receive grant funding from international foundations to create more jobs. Still others have volunteered to serve as consultants for your efforts to export your freshwater fish products to Europe."

You conclude, "Because Jesus Christ tells His followers to bless every people, we want to bless the Bozo people of Mopti."

Imagine the elders frowning at your offer. They ask, "And will you at the same time be telling them about Christianity? We are not Christians here; we are Muslims, and some worship the old spirits."

You reply, "We could have an agreement. We will do our very best to bless the Bozo people. If anyone asks why we are doing these things, may we tell them about Jesus Christ?"

The elders turn to each other slowly, faces inscrutable.

Finally one says—speaking English for the first time without translation—"Okay."

Next Steps

What's next for you? Blessing Bozos?

If you've been even slightly rattled in our study together, it might mean you look a little differently on the years between now and 2020, between now and the day you enter in through the gates of your celestial city, bearing the honor and glory of your people.

The "rattled" feeling might be tremors from your comfort zone. In any time-management, goal-setting, or personal-growth training your comfort zone is a key issue. In an uncertain world, where almost all we hear is the bad, terrorizing news and nothing of God's excellent deeds among the nations, it's easy to back into the personal safety of a predictable secure lifestyle. The last thing we need in our lives is discomfort.

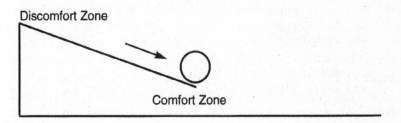

Most of us came to Christ because of some discomfort. Saying yes to His lordship was in many ways very easy—like a ball rolling downhill. We responded to the comfort of the Comforter, being accepted in the Beloved, sensing peace with God, and looking forward to an eternity of blessing in Zion. And most of us got plenty of support from fellow Christians about this new spiritual comfort zone. Fitting in with the consensus of the Christians around us brought even more acceptance, security—and eventually, predictability. (We know exactly how many verses of a song will be sung every week, we know all the right phrases, and our schedule revolves around the routine of the Christian gatherings we attend.)

But then Jesus comes up with His discomforting sayings, such as, "If anyone wishes to come after Me, let him deny himself and take up his cross, and follow Me" (Mark 8:34) and "If you want to be complete, go and sell your possessions and give the money to the poor" (Matthew 19:21, paraphrased). He calls us to a position of unpredictability, to a lack of practical security, a breaking from the herd—to a stance that is usually even more discomforting than before we knew Him!

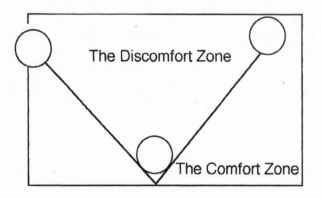

But now it's discomfort *with a purpose*. It's the adventure of a life on the edge of faith.

Surrendering our lives to Jesus Christ as Lord (Romans 10:9–10) is a no-strings-attached deal with God. So expect it—throwing our hands up in absolute submission to a Master who just might send us to Inner Mongolia or shift our prayer habits is discomforting! And yet that's precisely where we start in finding our part in God's cosmic plan. We stand before Him stripped of every self-induced security, yet comfortable in Him, trusting Him to be true to His character. And we simply follow Mary's advice: "Whatever He says to you, do it" (John 2:5). What's He going to say?

Finding Your Niche

God wants you to deeply understand the basics that He's already revealed. In fact, He probably won't get specific about where you fit now until you position yourself in what the Word teaches about the following steps:

Finding Your New Niche

Your Priesthood
As a priest, get good at interceding for and serving others: "But you are a royal priesthood" (Exodus 19:5-6; 1 Peter 2:9).

Your Life Experience
"Know Thyself." Think through God's design of your life as He uses everything you are—your heredity, environment, experiences, temperament, strengths and weaknesses: "I am fearfully and wonderfully made. . . . In Your book were all written the days that were ordained for me" (Psalm 139:14, 16).

Your Gifting
Study the spiritual gifts and determine yours: "There are varieties of gifts" (1 Corinthians 12:4).

Your Ministering
Practice your gifts in various types of service: "There are varieties of service" (1 Corinthians 12:5).

Your Impact
Explore various settings—including other cultures—for your ministering: "There are varieties of activities" (1 Corinthians 12:6 ESV).

Your Assignment
At this point in narrowing down what God has for us, He gets specific. Be alert to recognize what God has already planned for you to do: "He creates each of us by Christ Jesus to join him in the work he does, the good work he has gotten ready for us to do" (Ephesians 2:10 THE MESSAGE).

The Call

Often Christian organizations and churches talk of "a call" to certain ministries—especially ministries in another culture. Of course, God can call anyone to any task—through obvious circumstances, through mature advisors, through Scripture. He can call down through the clouds, speak through a donkey, or from a burning bush, to audibly clue in a follower to her or his place of ministry. But nowhere in Scripture do we find that a dramatic "call" is a doctrine or a requirement to move out in ministry.

The common idea is that you gain maturity as a believer, coming to some level of all-out commitment, and then you get a sort of supernatural call that tells you what you'll do.

The Bible does mention that individuals can be called to a particular life situation such as being single or married (1 Corinthians 7). But most uses of the word *call* in the New Testament refer to God's calling us to salvation. (See, for example, 2 Thessalonians 2:13–14 and Hebrews 3:1.)

The typical proof-text that believers have to wait for a "missionary call" to explore cross-cultural ministry is Acts 13:2: "Set apart for Me Barnabas and Saul for the work to which I have called them." Yet Paul and Barnabas were *already* ministering cross-culturally in Antioch when this direction came. Philip was already ministering cross-culturally in Samaria when God told him specifically to go to Gaza (Acts 8:26). When His harvest workers are already moving out in ministry, God does often fine-tune their directions: "Your ears will hear a word behind you, 'This is the way, walk in it,' whenever you turn to the right or to the left" (Isaiah 30:21).

Some say that Peter's vision to allow the Gentile house of Cornelius to hear the Good News was a call to missions. But, following that, Peter didn't then focus on a lifelong ministry among the Gentiles. Actually, Peter's vision was simply God's vivid reminder to bless *all* the nations (Acts 10).

Paul himself is the one New Testament believer who at the point of salvation was told he would go to the nations (Acts 26:15–19). This was not a specific call (Remember, there were 59,999 Gentile nations at that point!), but a call nonetheless. Yet Paul's singular, spectacular salvation experience with its mandate to take the Gospel to the Gentiles isn't a biblical doctrine.

The word *leading* might be more appropriate than the loaded word *calling* when it comes to God's specific role for you in His grand purpose. Mission scholar Herbert Kane interviewed hundreds of missionaries and found that although most spoke of a definite "call," upon careful evaluation most admitted that what they felt was a process of God's leading. For most, God's leading into missions took place over many years; for 80% of the interviewees that leading began when they were between ten and twelve years old! Kane determined the process was:

Curiosity: What is this people group like? Where do they live?

Interest: I want to keep learning more.

Understanding: I'm beginning to get a heart for this people.

Assurance: I believe God could use me in this group.

Conviction: I'm virtually designed to minister among this people.

Commitment: As God leads, I'm ready to engage in ministering to this people.

Action: I'm being confirmed as one to minister among this group.

Being *led* by God is biblically accurate and crucial; not moving till we get an experience-based "call" is suspect. Insisting on a specific supernatural call before engaging in global-scope ministry—when God's Word doesn't insist on it—often brings comparison, confusion, frustration, and guilt. We as God's people have been very clearly commanded and commissioned. We are to align our lives with God's objective of making follower-learners (disciples) of every people, including our own. In Old Testament parlance, we're to bless every nation, gracing them with the privilege of joining God's family through redemption in Jesus Christ.

Why all these disclaimers about a "call" to missions? Is that what *2020 Vision* is about? Recruiting missionaries?

Well, yes and no. If God leads you into an assignment of ministering cross-culturally, super. If not, it's still crucial to realize that a supernatural call isn't required to align every facet of your life with God's purpose—which happens to involve every culture on the planet! This is not about special Christians getting called; it's about *all of us being led.* It's about finding our life-purpose in the biblical, historical, cultural, and strategic plan of God.

Before we overview some suggested next steps for you personally: Remember your primary mandate to serve as a priest? It wasn't just given to you as an individual; you're part of a whole, holy *nation* of priests!

Rocket Science

How does your whole fellowship—all those fellow priests who worship with you—serve the purpose of God in their generation?

God fortunately didn't write the Bible in 100 topical sections. If He had, most of us would promptly turn to the topic that interests us most and neglect the rest. We might excel in understanding the eschatological ramifications of the hypostatic union of Christ but never browse through the section on washing one another's feet.

God didn't organize the Word with one section of study on His heart for blessing the nations; instead, He integrated that unchangeable purpose into passages dealing with His character, obedience, blindness, the meaning of the Incarnation, the growth of the church, and so on. So the idea is this: Don't concentrate on your interest in, say, reaching the Bozos of Mali and conclude that the rest of the church must then forget about discipling a younger brother, righting injustice, studying the Word, and feeding the homeless.

God's great purpose incorporates every God-given discipline in your life—and every ministry in the life of your church.

Think through these illustrations of the overall mission of a church. The local church is like a four-stage rocket!

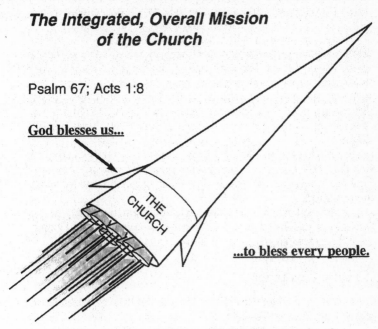

**The Integrated, Overall Mission
of the Church**

Psalm 67; Acts 1:8

God blesses us...

THE
CHURCH

...to bless every people.

The First Dynamic: God blesses His people to strengthen the church.

The church is to be strengthened for its task of channeling God's blessing to every people. Children need nurture in the admonition of the Lord, and families need encouragement and equipping in everything from communication skills to financial management. Couples must be counseled, youth discipled, offerings collected, prayers offered in behalf of the fellowship, bodies exercised, sermons preached, walls painted, fellowship enjoyed, buildings built, etc. All the gifts, skills, and ministries that go on within the church itself can be affirmed and encouraged because the church needs to be strong for its world-class purpose. This is the power dynamic, the "booster stage" of the rocket.

For example, let's say God has gifted and interested several people in your fellowship to minister to the elderly shut-ins of your congregation. Rather than chastise such folk that they should instead be polishing pith helmets bound for Bhutan, think integration: Perhaps God has blessed your church with a growing population of the very elderly. Why? Why hasn't He simply begun to take them home to heaven as He did during the first century when the average life-span was twenty eight? Clearly, God is blessing the elderly with time, with old age, for His great unchangeable purpose.

When your church's shut-in visitation team visits to share songs, hold hands, and listen to reminiscences, they can bring specific prayer requests of the urgent needs of the unreached peoples of the world. They can school the elderly in how to pray against the strongholds of Satan over a particular people group your church and mission is targeting. The team can infuse into each shut-in's remaining days the magic elixir of purpose: "You can spend time in prayer that we can't! You know more about the ups and downs of life than we do; you can pray specifically for the ups and downs of the mission team targeting this unreached group. You can help break open the way for the Gospel in this group as you pray against the principalities and powers that rule and blind them! We need you!" A church shut-in ministry can—and must—be incorporated into the vision of Christ's global cause.

Church ministries that help families and marriages get healthy are worthwhile not so much so we can be happier, but rather to keep us from being derailed from our part of His plan. Promoting physical fitness among believers has a big-picture purpose: to keep us from being distracted through health problems, or weary from being out of shape, as we pour our energies into our niche in His countdown to reach every nation.

Training in our finances has implications for the big picture of God's work too. Prayer sessions in the church don't have to center around pleas for more blessings for ourselves; they can be the classic times in which we agree together to bind Satan's power over a people (even our own), to open blind eyes and deaf ears to the Gospel, to corporately strengthen those we are sending to the front lines.

Every God-ordained ministry that strengthens believers within the church can be expanded as it aligns its purposes with the purposes of God.

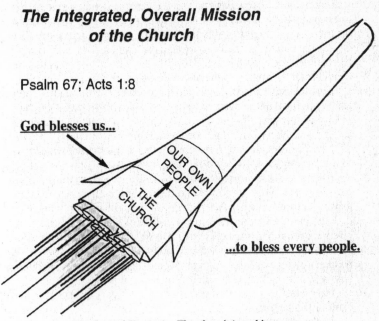

The Integrated, Overall Mission of the Church

Psalm 67; Acts 1:8

God blesses us...

OUR OWN PEOPLE

THE CHURCH

...to bless every people.

The Second Dynamic: The church is to bless every people group—including its own.

Here's where the church starts impacting the world outside its walls. Here is also where many mission fanatics fail in developing an *integrated* vision of God's heart for every people. Every people includes our own!

The easiest people group to offer God's blessing is, of course, a fellowship's own people group; we even know the language! Here are some ways this dynamic of the overall mission of the church can be expressed as salt and light:

In ministering to community needs Ministering goodness within a fellowship's own culture isn't simply a matter of being nice. Caring for the homeless, visiting the sick, ministering to those in prison, tending suicide hotlines, giving to the poor, sponsoring a single mothers' home, cleaning up trash on the highways, offering free baby-sitting for mothers' days off, raising money for medical research, singing Christmas carols in the mall—these all are ways of blessing one's own culture by simply going about "doing good" (see Acts 10:38).

The benefits of living in a community where Christians are consistently and sacrificially doing good makes visible God's love for humankind (see 1 John 4:1–12). God relieves suffering through His people. But further, Christians ministering goodness in the name of Jesus Christ illustrates the character of God for the whole world to see. Besides, serious Christian love in action makes a pleasant place to live for everybody, including Christians!

Caring ministries performed by believers impact a culture and a community in far-reaching ways. They witness to the culture and often set the stage for evangelism. They are, furthermore, a witness to internationals living in the church's culture and to the nations beyond. This is one of the reasons for obeying God: "Observe them [God's laws] carefully, for this will show your wisdom and understanding to the nations, who will hear about all these decrees and say, 'Surely this great nation is a wise and understanding people'" (Deuteronomy 4:6 NIV).

Before button-holing people with evangelistic threats of hell-fire we need to listen to God's desire to carefully evidence His character: "He has told you, O man, what is good; and what does the LORD require of you but to do justice, to love kindness, and to walk humbly with your God?" (Micah 6:8). Non-Christians ("pre-Christians") may not believe in absolute truth or creationism or moral values or churches. But they know genuine goodness when they see it, and the demonstrated good character of God wins a hearing for evangelism.

In evangelism As a church movement is established in a people group, it is that church's obligation to evangelize its own culture. So mass and personal evangelism isn't just one of the compartments of a local church's ministry; sharing the Good News with neighbors is crucial to the global scope of the Great Commission.

Standing up for righteousness in one's own people group This is another ministry category of this second dynamic of the mission of the church. A church must often bless its own culture the hard way—by taking a stand for God's character on issues.

When Christians fight pornography and immorality, battle drug abuse and child abuse, crime and corruption and injustice, they do more than help bless their own culture. God "guides [us] in the paths of righteousness for His name's sake" (Psalm 23:3).

God is holy, righteous, and just. So standing up for His name on issues in a believer's own society isn't just so the streets will be safer and life will be better. Blessing one's own culture by resisting unrighteousness also broadcasts to every people on earth the character of God. Every ministry of the church that presses against injustice, inequality, oppression, and sin in society is crucial to the global reputation of our righteous God.

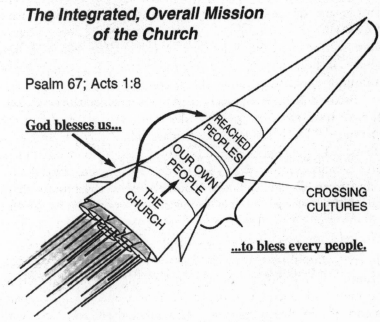

*The Third Dynamic: The church is to bless every
people group, including reached peoples.*

Here is where the church begins to cross cultural barriers. A "reached people" is a distinct ethnic group that has a viable church movement capable of evangelizing its own culture. About half of the people groups on earth are in this category.

A fellowship's ministries in this third stage are cross-cultural—that is, they must bridge language, social, or other cultural barriers. It is the job of the church in a reached culture, such as the Romanian culture (more than 12% are evangelical Christians), to bless its own people in evangelism and by doing good and standing up for righteousness in its society. So it is more than patronizing when another culture's church—a church from another reached people—tries to single-handedly do those jobs. It is actually offensive, since the outside culture is suggesting the people group's church isn't capable of evangelism, doing good, or salting its own society.

Barging in to do the work of another culture's church is also counter-productive to the pattern of God's global plan, since the church in a reached people will not grow strong if someone else is doing its work. And churches in reached people groups need to be strong (Dynamic #1) because they too have a global, big-picture job to do.

Blessing other reached peoples isn't about doing their ministry for them. It entails

- serving to help strengthen their churches (their Dynamic #1);
- facilitating—only as needed—their early work to bless their own culture (their own Dynamic #2) and to equip other reached peoples (their own Dynamic #3); and
- partnering with them to offer Christ's redemption to unreached peoples of the earth.

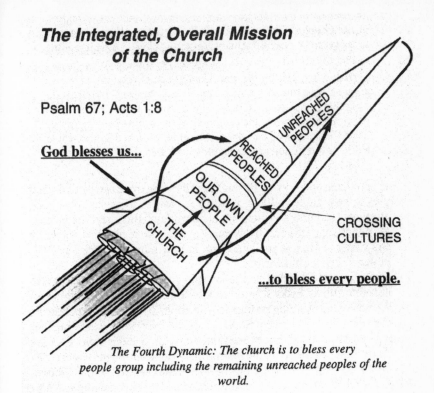

The Integrated, Overall Mission of the Church

Psalm 67; Acts 1:8

God blesses us...

THE CHURCH
OUR OWN PEOPLE
REACHED PEOPLES
UNREACHED PEOPLES

CROSSING CULTURES

...to bless every people.

The Fourth Dynamic: The church is to bless every people group including the remaining unreached peoples of the world.

The fourth dynamic of a church is to see that the blessing of redemption is offered to every remaining unreached people group. This is the realm of frontier, pioneer missions, where the entire church worldwide can partner to focus its resources. What happens in this stage of the "rocket" of the church?

Pre-Evangelism Pre-evangelism—relief efforts, Christians winning favor in political, educational, or business realms, medical work, etc.—is needed to prepare the way, to establish the reputation of the character of God in Christ among that unreached people.

Church-Planting Unbelievers come to faith in Christ, and churches are planted. Those newborn congregations are discipled to be strengthened, reaching out into their own people and crossing cultural barriers in their own process of being blessed to be a blessing to every people.

The whole church, with all its varying parts, functions,

giftings, and ministries working in unity, goes about the Father's business. We're not just a family; we're a family business, and so we have different roles, different departments, and different activities, but we're all in this together. God pours His blessing into us to pass on His blessing in Jesus Christ to the whole world—people group by people group.

Malfunctions in the Mission

The image of the rocket representing the mission of the church is, of course, faulty because being blessed to bless every people is not a chronological process. That brings us to the first of the possible malfunctions in our mission:

Sometimes we think any attention paid to the uttermost parts of the earth has to wait until we've first perfected our Jerusalems, Judeas, and Samarias. Although it's true that the stage-one blessing-strengthening of the local church is foundational to ministry, it's not true that we can't concern ourselves with other cultures until our own is fully redeemed.

Jesus told us to be witnesses *both*—simultaneously—in Jerusalem, Judea, Samaria, and the uttermost part of the earth (Acts 1:8).

Another malfunction in our mission can be getting stuck in the First Dynamic. A fellowship that concentrates on strengthening itself for the sake of strengthening itself is like a body builder who pumps up and pumps up his muscles—until he can hardly move.

A church that concentrates only on stage one is like the powerful booster stage of a rocket with no place to go. The first stage blasts into action and careens in every direction like a deflating balloon. A church with no clear direction but lots of activity diffuses its resources; the people tire of activity and suffer burnout. Ministry activity—virtually all within the fellowship—is furious, but the fruit of ministry is sparse.

Without a clear vision of their overall mission, of where they're heading, the people lose discipline. Without a vision, the people lose focus. As the King James version puts it, they perish (Proverbs 29:18).

Yet another malfunction of our single-vision mission is neglect of the First Dynamic. A fellowship might be excited about ministry outside the church but neglect to strengthen its base. That congregation might be like a needle-nosed rocket nosecone floating wonderfully through space with lots of vision and a sense of direction—but no thrust.

Often mission activist groups feel a clear sense of purpose and direction but are frustrated by lack of prayer power, financial power, and manpower. If the overriding problem for reaching out to a church's community or to another culture is the lack of resources, put it down somewhere: *You need a strengthened church.* You need to affirm and encourage the various ministries, to work at integrating a vision of God's purpose within every God-given ministry in the church.

A mission-minded church might malfunction by failing to impact its own culture in the Second Dynamic. What, then, gives it a right to tell an unreached people "blessed is the people whose God is the Lord"?

Look again at the scene that opened this chapter—you among the Bozos. A church with a vision of its mission that reaches to the uttermost parts of the earth must have a strong Second Dynamic. Fulfilling your obligation to bless your own culture gives the credibility that too often missionary enterprises lack in offering God's blessing to an unreached people.

Besides, if a local fellowship isn't evangelizing its own community, eventually it won't have enough prayer power, manpower, and other resources to be effective in the big picture. No new believers in the church is a sure sign of a malfunction. A mission-minded church that isn't activating its local ministries is destined to talk big but accomplish little in God's great global enterprise.

Running With the Vision

Pray through the following suggestions of how you personally can pick up this 20/20 vision of God's purpose for the nations—and run with it!

"Record the vision
And inscribe it on tablets,
That the one who reads it may run"
(Habakkuk 2:2).

Commit Yourself

- Write a letter to a distant best friend telling of your commitment to the vision of God's great purpose on earth.
- Explore your role as a "priest" (1 Peter 2:9–10). How can you literally or figuratively perform your priestly duties for your own people and other peoples of the world? The consecration rites of the sons of Aaron lasted seven days. What could you do daily for a week that would cement in your memory the fact that you are one of a people of God's own possession, a holy nation, a kingdom of priests?
- List your top-line blessings and pray/meditate on how you can consecrate each one as a bottom-line blessing. Your life is a big "reception": What do you have that you have not received (1 Corinthians 4:7)? Pray about how these blessings can be channeled into God's unchangeable purpose:

  - Spiritual gifts
  - Ethnic heritage
  - Big events that have shaped you (even negative events)
  - Education
  - Family traditions
  - Physical skills, talents
  - Supportive friends

- List activities you can do away with to better commit your time to God's purpose.
- Consider signing what is known as the "Caleb Declaration" of commitment:

  "Then Caleb quieted the people before Moses and said, 'We should by all means go up and take possession of it, for we shall surely overcome it'" (Numbers 13:30).

By the grace of God and for His glory, I commit my entire life to obeying His commission of Matthew 28:18–20, wherever and however He leads me, giving priority to the peoples currently beyond the reach of the Gospel (Romans 15:20–21).

As an expression of my commitment, I will attempt to fulfill the following:

1. I will go to another culture or stay in my own, depending on the Lord's leading.

2. I will share my vision with other Christians, recognizing that my local church or campus student group are the obvious places for me to begin.

3. To help me follow through with my commitment, I will "report" to someone—perhaps my pastor—monthly on how I am building and acting on this vision to reach every nation.

Signature _____

Date _____

(Consider photocopying this declaration and posting it where you'll see it often.)

- Raise a monument to your commitment. (See Joshua 4.) Actually build a monument (a pile of stones? a plaque? a slab of wet concrete?) to acknowledge your determination to align your life with God's unchangeable purpose; then annually spend a full day commemorating and renewing your commitment.

- If there is a possibility of your going to work cross-culturally here or abroad, connect with groups mobilizing the Harvest Force. A student-slanted Web site—*www.TheTraveling Team.org*—and a site for older adults—*www.Finishers.org*—will encourage you to progress in your commitment levels. Your favorite mission agency and your denomination will also have good resources.

Pray

- Put a sticky label-dot on your watch, your clock at home or work, and/or your car's rearview mirror to remind you to pray for the Lord of the harvest to thrust forth laborers.

- Communicate your commitment to pray for your church and denominational department or the mission agency you support.

- Look back at the list of people groups in chapter 2 or go to *www.joshuaproject.net/index.php* on the Web and list two or three unreached peoples to pray for. Don't worry that you probably don't know any specifics about these groups yet; God knows exactly who you're interceding for as you pray for these individuals and against the spiritual darkness over them.

- Subscribe to the *Global Prayer Digest*. Buy *Operation World: A Day-to-Day Guide to Praying for the World*. (See Resources.)
- Set up a system to remind you to intercede for the nations—your own included. It can be as simple as a card or sticky note listing your own people, a reached people, and an unreached people group—to prod your prayers while you are brushing your teeth, doing dishes, taking a shower, jogging, etc.
- Pray for a different unreached people group each day. Once a month pray for them all at once, finding their locations on a world map. Perhaps "tithe" a Sunday and spend one-tenth of your day in prayer for the nations.

Study

- Begin to memorize some of the focal passages cited in this study. (See the "For Further Thought" segments at the end of each chapter for suggestions.)
- Evaluate your personal study Bible as to how many of your underlined passages are "top line" and how many are "bottom line." Begin to underline the passages that specifically refer to God's blessing for the nations.
- Go back over the Bible study sections of *2020 Vision* and take the time to study carefully the passages mentioned.
- Read your Sunday newspaper and a national or large metropolitan Sunday newspaper—and/or surf Web news sites—to notice the hot spots of global news. How could God be using this incident to further His unchangeable plan to bless the nations? Determine how much time you'll devote weekly to thinking through world news relating to unreached people groups.
- Read and jot findings in books that focus on unreached peoples and finishing the task. (See Resources.)
- Take the *Perspectives on the World Christian Movement* course. (See Resources for more information.)
- Subscribe to several mission magazines and newsletters. Many mission organizations distribute updates by e-mail. (See Resources for suggested "generic" periodicals.)
- Go to school. For information on schools offering various

mission training programs, send for a copy of the *Evangelical Missions Quarterly Guide to Continuing Education*, Box
794, Wheaton, IL 60189, USA.

Give Time

- Write to missionaries working on the front lines. Give personal news of the home front. Send the Sunday comics section of the newspaper or other section you know he/she
  may enjoy. Encourage. Don't expect an answer. Be cautious
  in writing to any missionary working in restricted-access
  countries; check with your mission agency for guidelines.
- Connect with a mission agency that wants to learn more
  about a particular unreached group, and clip newspaper and
  magazine references; copy Web articles about that people
  and its geographical area. Don't forget that many mission
  groups still don't share much information; and breakthroughs reported in one denominational newsletter might
  be exactly the information another denominational mission
  department desperately needs! Be the information link for
  your agency.
- Volunteer five hours weekly to your church, service/evan-
  gelism ministry organization, or mission agency.
- Volunteer to help in your local or regional international student ministry. Shock foreign students by showing interest
  not only in what political country they are from but what
  people group they are from. Remember, you may be hosting an international student who is from an unreached
  people. Perhaps that one student will be the key, the evangelist who will plant a church and foster a movement
  toward Christ in his or her own people group!
- Find out if there are internationals from unreached people
  groups working or living in your community. Remember
  that individuals from most Muslim, Hindu, and Buddhist
  peoples will be from unreached groups. Develop relationships with these internationals, realizing again that they may
  be precisely the one family God has ordained to carry the
  Gospel back to their homeland!
- Use your vacation time to help research an unreached people
  group or assist in pre-evangelism (relief work, literature

distribution, etc.) in a major city with unreached people communities. You could even do this somewhere overseas. Contact your unreached peoples-focused mission agency for opportunities.

- Draw a timeline of your life from birth to death. Number your expected days (Psalm 90:12), and consider tithing a tenth of your expected lifetime to be involved full-time in sending or going. (With all we've studied, are you still waiting for a dazzling "call" from heaven?)

- Contact a mission agency targeting unreached peoples and start corresponding about possible short-term or career assignments.

- Research the possibilities of promoting missions in your area churches. Learn how to share the vision with groups. Encourage prayer, giving, and activism on behalf of the unreached. Contact your mission agency for ideas. (See Resources for "generic" mobilization ministries.)

Share

- Compile your list of top-line blessings and ask others for clues to other blessings you're not realizing in your life. You'll then have to explain the "blessed to be a blessing" principle!

- Find one or two friends who will meet with you for a regular (weekly? bi-weekly? monthly?) priestly prayer session for the nations. As you develop as a small group: Help each other clarify your motives in mission-interest; hold each other accountable for Bible study, prayer, and giving; encourage one another with global breakthroughs.

Enough ideas to prod your thinking? Your own response to the vision of God's orchestration of world events to proclaim His character to every people, tribe, tongue, and nation might never appear on such an action-step list. Remember the key: "Whatever He says to you, do it" (John 2:5)!

Live Long and Well

God is up to something wonderful in our day—regardless of the difficulties the future holds. A simple world population chart suggests that we need to be like the tribe of Issachar "who understood the times" and knew what God's people should do (1 Chronicles 12:32). The sharp upturn in our era disturbs many. But what could it mean in God's great historic plan? A massive harvest!

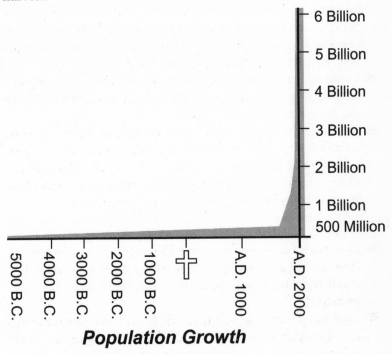

Population Growth

Perhaps part of understanding the times is remaining open to God's big-picture timing—to resist putting a date on when "this gospel of the kingdom will be proclaimed throughout the whole world as a testimony to all nations, and then the end will come" (Matthew 24:14 ESV).

Some Christians, worried that the world seems to be daily becoming a more dangerous place, gather tightly and simply hope that Jesus comes back soon—rather than moving, regardless of the challenges, into the harvest fields.

Yet God has His own schedule of when His plan will end (Acts 1:7). One clue that opens our thinking to a long life of serving as the nations' priests, to carefully passing on that responsibility to our children, grandchildren, and great-grand-children, is implied in God's own population chart. That is, He commanded the first earthlings and then Noah's family to "Reproduce! Fill the earth! Take charge! Be responsible for fish in the sea and birds in the air, for every living thing that moves on the face of Earth" (Genesis 1:28 THE MESSAGE; also see Genesis 9:7–9). Christian ecologists suggest that if we manage the earth's ecosystems responsibly as God commanded us, the planet is made to sustain a human population of perhaps 14 billion. Even with no major catastrophe on earth it will take hundreds of years for world population to "fill the earth." God just may prolong His intensive plan of making follower-learners of every nation (2 Peter 3:9) for many more generations. On the other hand, God tells us we have a part in "hastening the day" of His appearing (2 Peter 3:12). The mystery of God's timing reinforces the adage *Live as if He is coming back today; plan as if He is coming back in a thousand years!*

What does this mean for your life at this point in history? It means the harvest will continue to be plentiful. Come and join the reapers! And it means you can finish well—like your ancestor who first was blessed to bless all nations: "Abraham died in a ripe old age, an old man and satisfied with life; and he was gathered to his people" (Genesis 25:8).

Whether it's the year 2020, 2050, or beyond, your life, aligned with the solid purpose of God, will simply shine:

Arise, shine; for your light has come,
And the glory of the LORD has risen upon you.
For behold, darkness will cover the earth
And deep darkness the peoples;
But the LORD will rise upon you
And His glory will appear upon you.
Nations will come to your light,
And kings to the brightness of your rising.
Lift up your eyes round about and see;
They all gather together, they come to you. . . .
Then you will see and be radiant,
And your heart will thrill and rejoice!
(Isaiah 60:1–5)

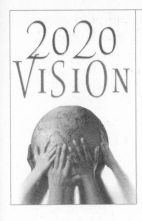

2020 VISION

RESOURCES FOR GROWING YOUR GLOBAL VISION

Note: Neither the authors nor the publisher endorses all the content of the following selected resources.

Books

Great, challenging reads on God's global perspective. Ask for the catalog.

Send the Light/William Carey Library
P.O. Box 1047
Waynesboro, GA 30830 USA
1–706–554–1594
Toll-free in the U.S.: 1–866–732–6657
www.gospelcom.net/wclbooks/
Gabriel@WCLBooks.com

Personal Studies

On-your-own courses to sharpen your part in the plan. Whether slanted toward younger or mature adults, the meat of these studies is applicable at any age. Each has accompanying lists of other key resources.

Look through the menu of resources under *Know Your World, Next Steps,* and *Beyond Urbana* at InterVarsity's *www.urbana.org.*

Excellent *12-Lesson* self-study on *Becoming a World Christian* from The Traveling Team at *www.TheTravelingTeam.org.*

Helpful info under *Starting Your Journey* for mid-life mission exploration at The Finishers' Project site *www.Finishers.org.*

Group Courses and Seminars

Integrate a vision of God's global purpose into your fellowship with resources that fit a Sunday school class, a home Bible study, a retreat theme, etc.

Solid Bible curriculum for a 12/13-week study, the Group Study Guide for *2020 Vision* is available at no cost at *www.BillAndAmyStearns.info.*

Perspectives on the World Christian Movement is the powerful course behind this book. Find a class offered near you:

Perspectives Study Program
1605 E. Elizabeth Street #1052
Pasadena, CA 91104–2721
1–626–398–2125
perspectives@uscwm.org
www.Perspectives.org

Perspectives has inspired several other resources. Contact the Perspectives Study Program office or look through the list at: *www.perspectives.org/include/psp_inspired_curricula.pdf.*

Prayer Guides

Operation World is an indispensable guide for global prayer. Order a copy at *www.OperationWorld.org* or at any bookstore: *Operation World,* Patrick Johnstone and Jason Mandryk, eds., Paternoster, 2001.

The *Global Prayer Digest* is a handy monthly guide to pray for the nations. Subscribe by phone at 1–626–398–2249 ext. 2249 or by e-mail for free daily prayer updates: Send an e-mail with no subject and no message to subscribe: *brigada-pubs-globalprayerdiges@XC.org.*

Or contact the Global Prayer Digest team at:
Frontier Fellowship—USCWM
1605 Elizabeth Street
Pasadena, CA 91104–2721 USA
www.global-prayer-digest.org

Other sources for worldwide prayer news in English are listed at *www.gmi.org/ow/resources/praypub.html.*

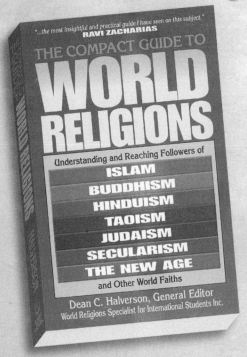